To the men and women who are serving and have served
in the armed forces of the United States of America...
and to their families.
Thank you for paying the price for our freedom.

Acknowledgments

To God. You're my best friend and my wise Counselor. Thank You for always being here for me.

To my prayer team. May God bless you for the hours you've encouraged me and prayed for me and this book. Thank you.

To those whose stories this book contains. I'm humbled that you trusted me to write your adventures. May you be blessed abundantly for sharing your hearts.

To Harvest House Publishers. I'm honored to be part of your family.

To Barbara Gordon. My bling sister. You're a tremendous editor, fun to hang out with, and a super friend. I'm looking forward to sharing more adventures with you!

To Tom Fox. As my daytime boss, thanks for "not noticing" my bloodshot eyes while I wrote this book and for your encouraging words. I appreciate you.

To Janet Kobobel Grant. You're an amazing lady, an incredible businesswoman, and a great literary agent. I thank God for you.

To my lumber customers and sawmill reps. Thank you for cheering me on. I cherish our friendships.

To all the horses, mules, dogs, and cats who have been my faithful companions. I thank God for creating you and putting you in my life.

Contents

A NOTE
FROM REBECCA

Horses! When I see these majestic creatures, they take my breath away. Their influence has changed the core of my being. They've taught me tidbits of wisdom on how to live a happy and successful life and the importance of cultivating a sense of humor. For a long time I thought I was the only one who felt this way, but I've discovered that's far from true. In these pages you'll meet incredible horses, along with a few other critters, and the people whose lives have been transformed by them. I pray these stories will encourage you to get to know Jesus Christ, help you live for Him, and empower you to reach out to others in His name.

May your life be richly blessed by God
as we saddle up and ride,

MEET REBECCA'S CRITTERS

· Dazzle ·

Dazzle is a beautiful Tennessee walker mare. One day when I'd traveled to a neighboring town to buy knobs for my kitchen cupboards, I happened to pick up a paper and saw an ad about her. I came home with a horse instead of knobs! Although she's bossy and keeps everyone in line, like a herd mare is supposed to, she's also kind and keeps me laughing with her sense of humor.

SkySong is my mainstay saddle mount. He's a tough, mountain-bred horse with a tender heart. I crafted his name especially for him. I love to pray when I ride, and prayer is a song in the sky to God—voila!—SkySong.

· SkySong ·

• Little Girl •

I bottle-fed *Little Girl*, my brown mule, because her jaw was broken when she was two days old. She was never supposed to live to be three days old—but I prayed and God answered. Now she's over 30 years old and enjoying retirement.

I planned *Wind Dancer*, my sorrel mule, from conception and talked with her while she was still in her mother's womb. I was thrilled when she was born, and she instantly knew who I was when she heard my voice. Currently she's my training project and an up-and-coming saddle mule.

• Wind Dancer •

• Sunrise •

Sunrise wriggled her way into my heart as a puppy. My fun-loving golden retriever loves romping behind me when I feed the horses and mules and trotting beside me when I ride the trail. She's so smart she taught SkySong to scratch her belly. Her boundless energy adds a zest to my days; and her soft fur makes a great foot warmer on winter evenings.

1

THE CLIPPER

Friendship

A light, spring breeze whispered past me, carrying the cool scent of snow down from the Rocky Mountain peaks that rimmed the Bitterroot Valley. I stretched the yellow extension cord across the winter-browned grass to the corral. My three horses and two mules were lined up at the gate begging for attention. They nipped at each other, trying to shoo each other away so the "top critter" could hog all the attention. My senior mule and my ancient horse sauntered to the other side of the corral to get out of the action. This day was "beauty parlor day." The mules would get their manes roached, and the horses would get their bridle paths clipped.

I picked up the large electric clipper to plug it in and noticed that SkySong, my dapple-gray horse, glanced at it and then walked away. I shook my head. I'd only owned him a few months. He'd been green broke when I bought him as a four year old. I'd wanted a horse whose bones and joints were fully formed before I asked him to scale tough mountain trails. And I wanted a horse that I trained. SkySong was perfect. Well, almost. Because his training started so late in life, he tended to be a bit snorty about some things. The electric clipper was one of them.

I pulled the halter off the wooden fence rail and walked across the corral toward him. He stopped and faced me. I slid the halter over his nose. Pushing his thick black mane aside, I buckled the halter behind his ears. "We're going to get you trimmed up."

Suspiciously his gaze darted to the side so he could watch me as I chattered. His feet clopped on the hard-packed dirt behind me as I walked to the gate. When I picked up the clipper, which I'd set on top of a tall, green trash can, SkySong threw up his head, his eyes focused on the dreaded equipment. The white whiskers on his muzzle stood straight out like porcupine quills.

I chuckled. "You silly boy. The clipper isn't even turned on. It can't hurt you."

SkySong wasn't impressed with my reassurance. When I held it out for him to smell, he clamped his nostrils shut and squinted his eyes.

I pulled the clipper away, and SkySong lowered his head and puckered his lips. I shifted my weight uneasily. *Lord, how is he ever going to get over this attitude?*

Reaching the clipper toward him again, I felt a nudge on my back. I turned. My black Tennessee walker had bumped my arm. "Dazzle, what do you want?"

She leaned her shoulder into me and arched her neck, as if asking me to clip her mane.

I patted her soft coat and laughed. "Okay, just a swipe for now." I clicked on the clipper. When it buzzed to life, SkySong threw his head up and snorted. Placing the clipper behind Dazzle's ears, I shaved off a small piece of mane just behind her ears.

I felt SkySong's breath on my neck. I glanced over my shoulder. He stared at me totally confused, almost as if he felt left out. He knew that the clipper was for him, so what was this clipping Dazzle all about?

With the clipper still buzzing, I turned toward him. He cocked his head and then stood still as I rested the cutter on his mane just above his withers and clipped a little bit of hair. Then I turned and clipped another piece off Dazzle. A nose nudged my back. I looked over my shoulder. It was my mule Wind Dancer. She stood on the far side of SkySong bobbing her head at me. The long winter growth on her mane flopped side-to-side. She too wanted her hair done. For the next 15 minutes I'd buzz a swipe off Wind Dancer's mane, then SkySong's, followed by Dazzle's. Back and forth I went until the job was done.

The first time this happened, I thought it was a novel experience. For the last few years, it's been the same—and not just with the clipper. No matter what SkySong's afraid of, his best friends come alongside him. I'm sure they're telling him, "See? There's nothing to worry about!" With a companion on each side, he draws from their strength and faces his fear.

What would happen if people did that for each other? If people are afraid of something, instead of teasing them, or telling them to buck up, or offering advice on how to solve the problem what if we came alongside and stood with them? Maybe all they need is a pat on the hand or a kind touch on the shoulder to remind them they're not alone.

One great example of this kind of friendship occurs between David, before he became king of Israel, and Jonathan, King Saul's son. "After David had finished talking with Saul, Jonathan became one in spirit with David, and he loved him as himself" (1 Samuel 18:1). Love bound the two together. Until Jonathan died, the two were like brothers. They believed in each other and helped each other through many trials.

From my animals to Jonathan and David, examples of true friendship are all around us. I want to be a true-blue friend who reflects God's love. How about you?

Lord, when my friends are experiencing difficulties, show me how to come alongside them without judgment and support them with love. Amen.

• Thoughts to Ponder •

Have you found that sometimes simply your presence is enough to give a friend the encouragement he or she needs? What meaningful ways have people encouraged you? Do any friends need you to come alongside them right now?

2

THE MISTAKE— HEAVEN MADE

God's Plan

The old, red pickup truck puttered down the Alabama highway. The muggy summer air blasted through the open windows, rustling Becky's long, blond hair. A couple times a week her daddy drove her out to a friend's farm where they pastured Becky's pony. Becky leaned forward as they passed the swampy area riddled with trees. Next was Boy's pasture. A barbed-wire fence surrounded the grassy field. Boy, an albino pony, was out in the field cropping grass. As soon as he heard the engine of their truck his head popped up. Spotting them, he gathered his haunches underneath him and raced toward the truck.

Becky couldn't imagine life without Boy. He'd become her physical therapist and most trusted friend. He'd shielded her from life's brutal storms. He was her miracle because he wasn't supposed be alive.

The truck slowed to turn through the opening in the fence. It rumbled over the cattle guard and bounced across the grassy two-track that led down to a weathered barn. They coasted to a stop as Boy skidded to a halt next to Becky's door. The truck door groaned as Becky flung it open and hopped out. The little pony stood perfectly still when Becky wrapped her arms around his neck and buried her face in his mane. She gave him a big, long squeeze.

Boy rested his head on her shoulder and drew the girl closer to him as if he were giving her a return hug.

For a moment Becky leaned into his neck, burying her nose in his fur. She drew a deep breath. She loved the way he smelled. She always felt safe when Boy gave her hugs. She looked up at the pony's eyes, reached into her pocket, and pulled out a soft peppermint stick.

Boy's eyes lit up. His whiskers wiggled as he caught a whiff of the sweet candy. Gently he placed his lips over the peppermint and took it from her hand. Becky giggled as he slobbered and smacked his lips. She remembered how she'd gotten him and what a miracle that was.

"A mistake." That's what Boy had been labeled. The colt of an unplanned pregnancy. The situation started shortly after her dad discovered his wife was pregnant with Becky. Her dad had stopped by to visit an old army buddy. Mr. John showed him a stunningly beautiful Tennessee walker mare and shared his high hopes. The mare was to be bred by a well-known Tennessee walker.

But as best-laid plans often go, the mare preferred the neighbor's Welsh pony.

As the pregnancy progressed, Mr. John was so upset that he threatened to kill the foal if it came out remotely resembling the neighbor's pony. Becky's dad loved horses and had raised and trained many. Although he was poor, he couldn't bear the thought of the foal being killed. He chimed in that if it looked like the Welsh pony, he'd take it.

Time went by, and Becky was born. Her leg was turned in at the hip, but the doctors weren't too concerned when she wobbled as she crawled. During the time Becky struggled to walk, her dad got the call from Mr. John. The foal was a blasted pony that looked like the Welsh sire. It was ready to wean, so if he wanted it he should come and get it right away.

Becky's dad put a rack on his pickup and took off. He brought home an albino Tennessee walker/Welsh colt. He started training the horse right away, and it was a good thing he did.

As Becky grew, her leg stayed canted to the side. She was taken to physical therapy regularly. One day at an appointment, her dad watched the doctor manipulate her leg. He cocked his head and asked, "Wouldn't horseback riding do the same thing?"

Becky's first memories are of her dad's strong arms lifting her on top of Boy's white, fuzzy back. She'd ride bareback and grab a fistful of Boy's long, white mane. Her dad would walk by her side and show her how to use her legs for balance and to steer the pony. By the time she started school, the hours of riding the pony had strengthened the muscles in her leg so much that it stayed straight unless she was tired.

Now, years later, Becky fondly remembers Boy. She still thinks of him as her own personal miracle. She marvels at God's planning. A Tennessee walker mare had fallen in love with an unlikely prospect—a Welsh pony stallion. The owner of the mare threatened to kill the newborn when her dad was around. Her financially poor father rescued it. Boy and Becky were born at nearly the same time. She needed physical therapy that Boy could provide. And most of all, she would need what the pony had to give—his love. Perhaps Boy had been a mistake by human standards, but Becky knows that by God's standards that pony was a great blessing He gave to her. Without a doubt, Becky knows Boy was born by God's design.

Blessings come from God. When I'm feeling discouraged, Becky's story gives me hope. If God plans when a horse is going to be born, surely He plans our lives. Can you imagine God watching someone being born and saying, "Wow, that's a surprise"? No, He's never said that. No one is a mistake. Even people born from "unplanned pregnancies" by human standards are planned and created by God.

Acts 17:26 reveals God's infinite design: "From one man [God] made all the nations, that they should inhabit the whole earth; and he marked out their appointed times in history and the boundaries of their lands." What a comforting thought! The God of the universe cares so much for us that He planned our lives before we were born. Like making sure Becky got her miracle pony, God is always at work around us crafting His wonderful plan.

Lord, reveal to me Your miraculous plans for my life. Amen.

• Thoughts to Ponder •

Have you doubted that you were created specifically by God and that you are part of His plan? Have you wondered if you should have been born? You don't have to wonder anymore! *You were planned by God!*

"You [God] created my inmost being; you knit me together in my mother's womb…Your eyes saw my unformed body; all the days ordained for me were written in your book before one of them came to be" (Psalm 139:13,16).

NIGHT RIDE

Finding the Way Home

Black...pitch black. The moon wasn't up, and not a star glimmered in the sky. The only sounds to be heard were the horses' metal shoes clicking against the granite on the trail and an occasional whisper of the wind through the pines. A cool breeze brushed past 10-year-old Shane, who sat in the saddle on his favorite horse named Paint. His dad was on a horse in front of him, and a friend and his horse were behind him. Shane could hear his dad's horse's hooves hitting the ground in front of him, but it was so dark he couldn't see the horse. He couldn't even make out a faint outline. The only way he knew which direction to go was by the sounds in front of him. His tummy churned. He didn't like riding blind.

Shane was already a good rider. He was growing up on a cattle ranch and spent his summers in the high mountains of California tending the herds. More than one night he'd ridden back to the ranch in the dark. But this was different. They were in the middle of the Yosemite Wilderness, 9000-feet above sea level. There were no neighbors' lights glimmering in the distance. Shane waved his hand in front of his face. He couldn't even see it. Worse yet, they were bushwhacking through downed timber and across granite slabs to ride back to their "spike," or secondary, camp.

They were on a guys' outing—a pack trip into the wilderness. That morning they'd tied their fishing poles onto their saddles and stuffed sack lunches in the saddlebags before riding out of their tent camp and winding up the steep mountain. They didn't follow a trail. They were exploring the area to find a hidden lake with crystalline blue water—a place they were sure no one had gone to before. The day had promised to be full of adventure, and indeed it had been.

They'd found the lake's general location, tied up the horses, and hiked in. Soon they had their lines in the water. While fishing around the granite shore, they'd killed two rattlesnakes that had threatened them. They had so much fun gawking at the trophy-sized trout and trying to catch more that they lost track of time. The sun was sinking low behind the sheer peaks when they folded up their fishing poles, hiked over the top of the mountain, and scaled down to the horses. They had just enough time to tie their gear onto their saddles and swing up before the sun fell from the sky and darkness engulfed them.

In the black night, Shane heard his dad's horse crash through some deadfall. Shane's dad gruffed a few words and then turned in the saddle and called back to his son. "Shane, get up here in front and drop the reins on ol' Paint. He's surefooted and will lead us back to camp."

Shane braced himself as he nudged Paint forward. He didn't want to be in the lead. He didn't know where to go. *Can Paint see where he's going? Will he step off the side of the mountain?* the boy wondered. When his dad rode in front of him, Shane could tell if the trail was going uphill or downhill by the sounds, but now he was on his own. He grabbed onto the saddle horn with one hand as Paint lurched around the other horse and moved into the black night. Shane felt his horse's back muscles ripple. Paint pulled on the reins and then dropped his head and snuffled the ground. Shane figured he was working out where they were. Paint suddenly raised his head and lengthened his stride. Shane's body rocked backward.

The boy's mind raced wildly. *What about the limbs on the trees? Will they whack me in the face and poke my eye out? Will a branch knock me out of the saddle?* Shane slowed his horse to a crawl. He wanted to hold an arm in front of his face, but he didn't want to let go of the saddle horn or the reins.

His dad's voice roared behind him, "Just let Paint have the reins!"

Shane knew that really meant "Get moving!" He felt like he was on a roller coaster with his eyes shut. He struggled to keep his balance when Paint stepped downhill. When the horse dislodged stones, Shane shuddered as he heard them drop off the cliff and ricochet to the bottom. Plink…plink…plunk. His heart pounded when he heard Paint's hooves scrape over the bark of a downed log. He forced himself to tie a knot in the reins and drop them on Paint's neck. An hour later Paint stopped. They'd arrived at their spike camp safe and sound!

Now, decades later, Shane remembers that ride as one of his most memorable times as a kid because he had to let go of the reins and trust Paint to take him home.

That reminds me of a time mentioned in the Bible. God told Abram to pack up and move. "The Lord had said to Abram, 'Go from your country, your people and your father's household to the land I will show you'" (Genesis 12:1). At that time Abram was no spring chicken. He was 75 years old! And God didn't give Abram specific directions, such as "Go until you get to the olive tree and take a left." God simply said, "Go."

I wonder if Abram had to fight thoughts of doubt? *But where, God? If I don't know where I'm going, how do I know what to bring?* How could a 75-year-old man tell his wife, his nephew, and his servants to pack all their stuff and go traipsing into the sunset? Or maybe it was the sunrise. Did he have a clue which direction to go before he got on his camel?

Like Abram and Shane, we need to let go of the reins of our daily lives. We need to let God guide us to where *He* wants us to go. He never promised to unfold His whole plan in front of us—probably because He knows us too well…He knows me too well. If I saw the whole plan, I'm sure that in 10 seconds flat I'd have everything organized into checklists. Before long it wouldn't be God's plan anymore.

God shows us the next step, and that's all He expects us to follow. We move forward one step at a time under His direction. That's why it's called *faith*. So if you're facing a dark night, pray. Ask God what your next step is, and then drop the reins, let God lead, and hold on for the ride of your life!

I'm so glad, Lord, that You can see into the future, that Your wisdom is perfect, and that You generously share Your wisdom with me. Please do that now. Amen.

· Thoughts to Ponder ·

Do you ever feel like you're riding a horse through the dark along the edge of a cliff? That at any moment you could plunge into an abyss? I encourage you to ask God to be your Guide and then drop the reins and follow Him. He'll get you home every time.

4

MISSING

Finding the Answer

My headlamp cast a narrow beam of light through the corral. Steam from my breath hung in the still, winter air. The black-plastic sled laden with hay bumped and scraped across the snow as I dragged it behind me. It was four in the morning and feeding time for my five horses and two mules. Two were seniors, so I'd worked out a special routine. I fed the young stock in the corral, and the ancient ones I fed in the pasture by themselves. That way the old ones could linger over their food for a few hours, chewing it slowly with their worn-down teeth. If I didn't separate them for feeding, the young ones would gobble down their food and push the old ones out of the way and scarf down theirs too. Just before leaving for work, I'd put them back in the same pasture.

The squeaking sounds of hooves in the snow followed closely behind me. My mind swirled with all the decisions I needed to make. Over the past few weeks I'd been trying to figure out if I should sell my pickup truck and buy a new one. Mine was old and needed some work done to it. I'd asked my family and friends for their opinions. I'd even looked at some of the used car places and read the classifieds looking for another truck. One minute I wanted a new-to-me truck; the next minute I'd wonder if I should fix mine. I couldn't make up my mind.

I tossed a couple flakes of hay into a wooden feeder. In the shadows caused by my headlamp beam, I saw Dazzle and Wind Dancer belly up to the feeder. When I grasped the rope on the sled and pulled it forward, it sounded like only two animals were following me. I turned and cast the beam of light around. Sure enough, one was missing—Czar. I'd owned him since he was a colt, and he'd never missed out on a meal.

Something must really be wrong, I thought. He'd been my saddle horse in the mountains, and I'd ridden him thousands of miles. He'd been my best friend and had saved my life a couple times. At 31 years old, he was fading away. With a heavy heart, I swung my head back and forth, shining the light around the corral to look for him.

Nothing. *Maybe he went out into the pasture. Maybe he lay down and died. It's about his time. When it gets to be daylight, I'll go look for him.* My heart was heavy as I fed the other two critters and dragged the sled back to the barn. As I entered the narrow doorway, out of the corner of my eye I glimpsed something. I jumped, gasped, and turned my head to aim the light on it. I laughed! Czar stood next to the large stack of hay, his back sagging from his years. He turned his head and blinked. Stems of alfalfa stuck out from between his lips. He was eating the hay directly out of the bales! In all the years I'd owned him, he'd never gone into the barn willingly. I slipped a halter on him. "So, the wise old horse goes right to the unlimited source now," I said with a smile as I patted his neck.

· Czar and Rebecca ·

I giggled as I led him out to the pasture. *That's exactly what I need to do too,* I thought. *Go to the unlimited Source of all wisdom.* Although it was good to have asked for people's opinions about buying a different truck, I realized I'd never asked God! The next few days I invested time in prayer. I sensed I was to get my old truck fixed. That was several years ago, and I'm glad I did. I still have the same truck, and it's perfect for me.

Czar lived another year. Over the many years we traveled life's trail together, I learned so much from him. On that "going to the Source day," God showed me such a huge message through Czar. Even though it may seem like such a small thing, it was life changing because it reflected God's wisdom: "If any of you lacks wisdom, you should ask God, who gives generously to all without finding fault, and it will be given to you" (James 1:5). God provides road markers for walking out a life of faith. I've not deliberated long over decisions since then because the all-knowing God of the universe is more than willing to share His wisdom. It's sometimes hard to wait for His reply, but it always comes.

Lord, when I forget to ask You for wisdom,
please nudge me. Amen.

· Thoughts to Ponder ·

Do you get so consumed in gathering information to make a decision that you forget to ask God what would be best for you? Are you facing any decisions now? What steps will you take to consult the ultimate Source of wisdom?

5

ALL WET

Obedience

The purple light of dawn was breaking across the Cypress Hills in Saskatchewan, Canada. Most of the snow had melted, filling the creeks to their banks. A whisper of nippy air hung over the rolling hills. Ross grabbed a halter and walked into a large calf pen. In the dim morning light, he cast a glance over the large pasture. He'd put a lone saddle horse in here last night so they could get an early start. He called, "Brandy! Come 'ere, Brandy!"

Today Ross was headed over to the neighbor's place to help them brand calves. It was going to be a long, sweaty day so he'd chosen one of his favorite horses to ride. Brandy was a bay mare who had been born on his ranch and was worth her weight in gold. He'd trained her himself. One of the first things he'd taught her was to come when called. She'd turned out to be a cracking good partner for calving, irrigating, pulling calves close to the branding fire, roping, and trailing cattle in the hills. The wise horse had even helped teach Ross's children to ride. During the tough and long day of branding coming up, a good horse would make it much easier—almost pleasant.

Glancing around the pasture, Ross spotted Brandy down by the creek nibbling slender new shoots of green grass. Her fuzzy winter coat made her look blocky and stout. He cupped his hands to his mouth. "Come 'ere, Brandy!" With halter in hand, he walked toward her.

Brandy lifted her head. She watched him, but she didn't move.

When Ross stepped across the brown grass near her, she zeroed in on the halter. Ross called, "Come on! We've got work to do."

Brandy wasn't interested in work so she did a shocking thing. She whirled away from Ross and leaped toward the creek. She obviously expected to land on ice, which she'd been walking on all winter, and scamper to the other side. But the ice had thawed, and she hadn't been in this pasture long enough to notice. She landed in a deep pool. The flood-stage creek completely swallowed her. She disappeared from sight—ears and all!

In a millisecond, she bobbed to the surface, scrambled to the bank, and heaved herself up on dry ground. Her ears flopped to the sides as water gushed off her. The mare shook and then sheepishly walked over to Ross.

He burst out laughing.

Looking guilty, she planted herself in front of him and rolled her eyes as if to say, "Sorry, boss. I really didn't mean to act like that."

Ross chuckled as he scratched her neck for a few minutes. He haltered her, led her to the driveway, and loaded her in the horse trailer. He drove to the neighbor's place, unloaded his horse, and saddled up. The two had a great day at the branding.

I laughed when Ross told me about Brandy and her willful disobedience. In my mind's eye I could picture water rushing off and out of her ears. Then I thought about another time, many years ago, when disobedience caused a human to get all wet. In the Bible, the book of Jonah contains the historical account of one of God's prophets—Jonah. Back in those days there was a city named Nineveh in which wickedness flourished. God told Jonah to go to that city to preach against evil and share His love. But Jonah didn't want to, so he acted like Brandy!

"Jonah ran away from the Lord and headed for Tarshish. He went down to Joppa, where he found a ship bound for that port. After paying the fare, he went aboard and sailed for Tarshish to flee from the Lord" (Jonah 1:3). Jonah thought he'd escaped and was safe in the boat bobbing around on the sea. Did he think God would forget about him or that somehow he'd become invisible when he boarded the boat? I don't know, but no matter how far he ran, God was watching Jonah from His vantage point in heaven.

To shake Jonah out of the boat, God sent an enormous storm that threatened to swamp it. Jonah confessed to the crew that the storm had come upon them because he was running away from God. The prophet told the crew to toss him overboard so the sea would become calm, but they refused. When the storm grew more violent, they asked God to not hold them accountable, and then they threw Jonah overboard. Instantly the storm ceased and the sea grew calm.

Out of His great love, God sent a big fish to save Jonah by swallowing him. For three days and three nights while inside the gurgling guts of the fish, Jonah had a chance to reflect on the stupidity of trying to run from God. "From inside the fish Jonah prayed to the LORD his God" (2:1). While still sitting in the dark amid the stinky gastric juices, the prophet praised God for saving him from drowning in the sea. Jonah said he would do as God asked, and tell the people in Nineveh that salvation comes from the Lord (2:8-9).

Shortly after that prayer, God commanded the fish to spit Jonah out on dry land. (That was a miracle in itself! The fish ferried him to shore!) I bet it wasn't long before Jonah took a bath and changed his clothes. Then he hotfooted it to Nineveh to preach the good news of salvation. The people repented and turned to God, and He relented and didn't bring destruction down on them (3:10).

I imagine that after sitting in the belly of a big fish with his knees knocking for three days, Jonah didn't try to run from God again! And after Brandy took her dive into the creek, she never whirled and ran from Ross again. Both of them were running out of willful disobedience, thinking only of themselves and what they wanted.

God doesn't call us to obedience for our own pleasure. His call is to take action and serve others. Jonah's obedience influenced more than 120,000 people to turn from their evil ways so God wouldn't destroy them (4:11).

Looking at Brandy's and Jonah's scenarios encourages me to consider how I respond to God. When He talks to my spirit, do I evaluate what He asks me to do based on what I want to do? Or do I say, "Yes, Sir!" and step out in faith by immediately doing what He's asked? I confess that I've responded both ways. I've even tried to hide from God. But how can I be invisible to the God of the universe, the One who sees all and knows all?

The wonderful news is that if I miss God's call to action, He, through His great grace and mercy, is willing to restore me as soon as I repent for not listening and then choose to walk with Him. Even if I willfully disobey Him, God is still willing to restore me when I repent, although I may suffer some consequences for not heeding Him.

In the long run, obedience is easier and much more fun than getting all wet.

Lord, when I'm tempted to ignore Your commands, please remind me that what You're asking isn't just about me. It's also about serving others in Your name. Amen.

• Thoughts to Ponder •

Has God asked you to do something, and you immediately ran the other way or ignored His command in another form? How did that work for you? Would you like to get in right standing with God? Simply ask Him to forgive you and guide you in the way He wants you to go.

6

IMPOSSIBLE PRAYER

Childlike Faith

The yellow, four-door, 1977 Chevy pickup belched smoke as it rattled into the driveway. The driver's door creaked as Lou pushed it open and unwound his six-foot frame to step out. He was looking forward to a few minutes to unwind and play with the kids before he began studying. Opening the front door, he could hear the children's laughter down the hall. After greeting his wife, he stretched out in his leather recliner and thought about how the last few months had been a blur.

God had put a call on Lou's life to become a minister, so he'd quit his well-paying job and enrolled in Bible college. He and his wife sold their beautiful home and, with their four children (ranging in ages from 6 to 12 years old), moved into a cookie-cutter-type house. Going to school and working a low-paying job tightened the purse strings. Sometimes there was more month than money.

Out of the corner of his eye, Lou noticed Liana, his eight-year-old daughter, briskly walking toward him like an attorney on an important case. Her jaw was set, making the dimples in her cheeks deeper. Lou knew there was an interrogation coming. Although amused, he kept a straight face. "What's up?" he asked.

With one hand behind her back obviously holding something, she framed her words. "Remember the discussion we had about the pony?"

Lou nodded even as "Oh oh" flashed through his mind.

Liana recounted the conversation and then presented her evidence. From behind her back she held out a piece of lilac-colored construction paper. Stars drawn with red-colored pencils adorned the corners. Unicorns galloped around the edges. In the center was a carefully trimmed newspaper ad. Her eyes twinkled. "I found a Shetland pony for sale." She handed it to her dad.

Lou hesitated as he glanced at it.

Liana squirmed.

Finally Lou broke the silence. "How much are they asking?"

Liana announced, "Two hundred dollars."

Lou shook his head. "That's way beyond our price range. Remember, we agreed to spend $125."

Pursing her dainty lips, she wielded the words he'd often used on her. "What do we have to lose by asking if they'll take $125?"

The pony dream had started in Liana's Sunday school class with a teaching on prayer, faith, and believing. After passing out white index cards and pencils, the teacher asked the children to write a prayer on something close to their hearts. She told them to take the cards home and believe that God would answer their prayers. Liana asked God to give her a pony.

When Lou came across the index card, he thought, *This is an impossible prayer. It's impossible because I've got four kids to feed, school to pay for, and a job that doesn't bring in enough money as it is.* The list of horse-related expenses would be endless too: saddle, bridle, blanket, halter, lead rope, hay, and a horse trailer. *And where would we put a pony?*

But the simplicity and innocence of Liana's prayer inspired him to show his wife. After praying they agreed on a plan. Gathering their four children around the dining room table, Lou and Sue shared that they were considering getting a pony. Amid all the excitement, Lou set down the conditions. "The most we can spend is $125."

In unison the children groaned. "But, Dad…"

Even the children knew that buying a pony for $125 in Southern California was a difficult task. Lou was adamant. "If it's God's will that we get a pony, He will have to be the One to make it happen." Lou closed the discussion with, "If you find a pony for that price, we'll go out and take a look at it." He didn't think it would happen.

Then Lou noticed Liana had taken an interest in reading the newspaper. In May she'd found this ad.

Lou held the lilac construction paper. He picked up the phone and dialed the number. After introducing himself, he explained, "I had to make this call because of my daughter's prayer. Do you mind if my wife and I come out and look at your pony for sale?"

The yellow pickup wheezed up the hill through the gated community. Lou chuckled as he shifted gears. *We must look like Ma and Pa Kettle,* he thought. Mansions were perched on 10-acre ranchettes. When Lou and Sue pulled into the driveway at the address given, they were greeted by a charming older couple who looked like Mr. and Mrs. Santa Claus. They were even plump, sported rosy cheeks, and had twinkles in their eyes.

They explained their grandchildren had outgrown this cherished pony, and now they were moving. They wanted the pony to have a family with children who would love him.

Strolling behind the barn to the back acreage, Lou and Sue glimpsed a very short palomino pony. Its long, cream-colored mane nearly buried its dark-brown eyes. Because Sue had grown up with horses, she gave Taffy the "kid-proof test." She rubbed Taffy's fuzzy coat all over, walked behind her, lifted her hooves, and even crawled under her belly.

Lou's mind whirled with "Cha-ching, cha-ching" as he thought of how much money a cash register would swallow when it came to buying tack and supplies.

After Sue nodded her approval, Lou confidently stepped forward and made the offer he knew they wouldn't accept. "How about $125?"

The couple shared that they'd had other people who had wanted to buy this pony. They'd turned them down because it hadn't seemed right. But it felt right to sell the pony to them. They accepted the offer.

Shocked, Lou stammered, "I–I…w–we don't have a place to keep her. Would it be okay if she stays here until I find a suitable pasture?"

The couple nodded. "She also comes with a halter, a bridle, grooming brushes, a saddle, and three bales of hay," the husband added.

A committee of four children lined up in the living room when Lou and Sue arrived home.

Trying to keep a straight face, Lou asked, "Guess what?"

The kids *tried* to remain quiet.

Lou smiled. "You guys own a pony!"

The children erupted with joy and cheers and hugs abounded.

The next day Lou and Sue took the kids out to see their new pony.

When Liana wrapped her arms around Taffy's neck and buried her face in its fur, it was love at first sight…It was a match made in heaven.

Liana's faith is what Jesus is looking for in us. Jesus shared His heart when He taught, "Truly I tell you, anyone who will not receive the kingdom of God like a little child will never enter it" (Mark 10:15).

Oftentimes I make faith too complex. If God wants us to be like children, He doesn't expect us to have all the answers or be "qualified" to approach Him. He wants us to come to Him with childlike wonder and expectant hearts because we believe what He says.

Liana's faith didn't just result in the family getting Taffy. Another miracle took place. While still on a tight budget, Lou and Sue managed to purchase 20 acres of land that included a makeshift barn and a pond. They put a small mobile home on it to live in, and they rented a U-Haul horse trailer to transport Taffy to her new home.

When Lou shared this story with me, he also handed me the "why" for the ability to purchase the land. It was an aged index card with a child's cursive writing on it: "I will pray for my family to get 20 acres of land and for us to be able to rent a horse trailer for Taffy."

God answered another "impossible" prayer by eight-year-old Liana.

Lord, when I come before You, remind me to leave the complexities of life behind and speak from my heart with the trusting faith of a child who loves You. Amen.

• Thoughts to Ponder •

Have you felt uneasy about praying because you feel you're not trained or qualified to talk directly to God? Is it hard to believe that He will listen to and answer your prayers? What does God's Word say about that?

7

A GOOD ROPE FOR ROUGH COUNTRY

Being Prepared

The soft plodding of the horses' hooves hitting packed clay hung in the warm, spring air. Twelve-year-olds Hillari and Laurie rode their horses on the hardpan trail along the banks of the Santa Ana River in Riverside County, California. Scrubby, six-foot-tall creosote bushes adorned with olive-green leaves on twisted gray stems dotted the landscape seemingly all the way to the distant mountains. The meager spring rains had passed, leaving behind tufts of green grass and the sweet-smelling leaves on the cottonwoods. The girls were headed home after a peaceful Saturday trail ride through the citrus groves.

Riding in the lead on her bay mare, Hillari wondered if they should take the cut-off trail home. It wound down a cut in the riverbank, across the riverbed, and up the bank on the other side. It was a trail they liked to take. She glanced at the wide and dry expanse. Months ago, during the winter and early spring rains, the river had raged. The water had risen quickly, cut into the steep banks, and washed away trees. It had eventually receded, leaving behind gravel and sandbars littered with branches and dead trees and occasional pools of standing water.

Hillari's body swayed with the rhythm of her horse's walk as she analyzed the trail. Fresh motorcycle tracks scored the path. *It must be safe to cross if the motorcycle riders are using it,* she thought. Turning in the saddle, she caught Laurie's attention, motioned toward the riverbed, and shouted, "The motorcycles are using it. What do you think?"

Laurie's stout buckskin gelding strode forward as his rider surveyed the trail. She nodded.

Hillari and Laurie had been riding together since they were five years old. Even though Laurie was an olive-skinned brunette and Hillari was a fair-complected blond, people thought the two tall, slim gals with waist-length, straight hair were sisters. The girls felt like they were sisters. They'd ridden together so much they could read each other's minds and complete each other's sentences. Their favorite thing to do was to pretend they were two cowgirl pioneers out on an adventure. Although they wore T-shirts and jeans, they looked the part of pioneers—sitting tall in their western saddles, their lariats coiled and tied onto the pommels of their saddles. They'd started carrying the lariats after an old cowboy had given one to Hillari, along with these words of wisdom: "A smart rider never rides through rough country without a good rope."

Hillari reined Farrih toward the riverbed. Bred to have the intelligence and endurance of an Arabian and the size and athleticism of a thoroughbred, the Anglo-Arabian mare gracefully headed down the slope. Shifting her weight to her hind legs, she half-shuffled, half-skidded down to the riverbed.

Laurie's buckskin gelding ambled behind. The sandy path wound through the river bottom. Halfway across the wide, dry riverbed a long, scrubby cottonwood branch blocked the trail. The skeletal arms of a gnarled limb stood too high to comfortably step the horses over without scratching their bellies. Without slowing, Hillari gently pressed her leg against Farrih, asking her to step to one side. Willingly the mare moved onto the sand about four feet off the trail.

Suddenly the mare pitched forward.

Hillari grabbed the reins. *What's going on?* The mare's front legs had sunk to her knees, followed by her hind legs. She snorted and half jumped trying to get out of the mire.

Hillari centered her weight to help the mare stay balanced. She firmly pressed a rein against her horse's neck, hoping to guide the mare to firmer footing. The girl's heart pounded as her mind flashed through scenes of movies that involved quicksand. *Quicksand!* That's it! Farrih had broken through the top crust of dried sand and sunk into a thick quagmire.

The mare lunged again. She broke through another top layer and sank nearly to her belly. Terrified, she swung her head, her eyes wide with panic.

Hillari gasped as her mind raced. *What do I do now? I've got to get my weight off Farrih so she doesn't break through another layer. Will the crust hold my weight?* She looked at the broken edges of the sand. She might be able to stand on the top. If not, it looked thick enough to support her weight if she spread it out by crawling on her hands and knees.

The mare's nostrils blew snorts of alarm. Sweat dribbled behind her ears and down her neck. Her muscles tensed as she prepared to lunge again.

Hillari had only a fraction of a second to act. Stroking Farrih's neck, she forced her voice to be calm. "Easy there." Quickly she swung a leg over the saddle.

The mare's gaze darted back at her, watching her.

Hillari gently but firmly commanded, "Whoa now." Balancing on her stomach on the saddle, she slid down and tested the firmness of the sand with her boots. It held. She lowered herself all the way to the ground. *It's only four feet back to the trail, and we'll be on solid ground,* she reassured herself. Clinging to the reins, she held her arms out to her sides for balance. She slowly shuffled, taking one step and then another.

The bay mare's eyes were bulging and her nostrils gaped for air. Struggling to follow, she threw her weight forward.

Hillari turned and looked into her horse's large, brown eyes. Reaching out she stroked the mare's face as she commanded, "Whoa, girl. Easy now. We'll get you out."

The mare froze in place, but her anxiety was clear to see.

Hillari glanced sideways at Laurie, who sat wide-eyed astride her horse, now about 12 feet in front of Farrih. "Stay on the path!"

Farrih's labored breathing reverberated over the sand.

Hillari's mind whirled. *How much time do we have before Farrih thrashes through another layer and sinks out of sight?* She sorted through the facts. There weren't any homes or buisinesses close enough to get help fast enough. If Farrih kept struggling, she'd overheat, go into shock, or sink more. Whatever was going to be done needed to happen now and by them.

Laurie called, "What can I do?"

Hillari slid her feet onto solid ground. Taking a deep breath, she continued to reassure her mare as she walked back to Laurie and stood next to the buckskin. The two girls formed a plan. They'd use their lariats to drag the mare out. It was dangerous because she might break her legs, but it was all they had.

Hillari crawled across the top of the sand toward Farrih. Damp sand stuck to her hands with each reach. Laurie's lariat hung in a coil around her neck. Her blue jeans wicked up water and were becoming heavy.

The mare's head was low, her chin resting on the crust of sand in front of her. Her eyelids fluttered and her ribcage expanded rapidly as she gasped for air. The horse's bay coat was spattered with sand. She opened her eyes and spotted Hillari. She plunged forward. Her feet churned but she wasn't able to get traction.

Hillari was scared. She wanted to shout at Farrih so she would stop moving. The mare could be cutting her tendons to shreds against the rough edges of the sand. Hillari knew if she raised her voice her horse would become even more upset. Choking sobs racked her body as she reached her hand forward and shifted her weight. Doubts assaulted her. *What if Farrih lunges and I get pulled underneath her?*

Sliding her knee forward another thought crashed through her mind. *What if Laurie's horse gets dragged into the sand with Farrih?* Hillari hesitated, carefully balancing her weight as evenly as possible. *We can't do this…I can't do this. But who else is there? Farrih's my horse. She's never let me down, and I can't let her down.* She swallowed hard, gathered all her courage, and crawled within three feet of the trapped mare. "Whoa, Farrih. Easy girl," she crooned.

Grayish-tan sand coated the mare's neck and sides. Her teardrop-shaped ears twitched as she watched her master. Sweat foamed behind her ears and rolled down her neck.

For an instant, the girl and her horse stared into each other's eyes. Hillari lowered her voice, gently murmuring, "Easy now, girl. Stand still."

The mare stilled, almost as if she understood.

Hillari crawled to Farrih's side and stroked her neck. Lying down and stretching out on her belly, she reached over the saddle and untied her lariat. Quickly she slid the loop end around the saddle horn and pulled it tight. Lifting Laurie's rope from her neck, she threaded it around the mare's head while whispering softly, "Easy, girl. I'm going to tie this up." Nimbly Hillari's fingers tied a knot that wouldn't tighten down and choke the mare. Holding the two ropes, she shinnied backward toward solid ground.

Suddenly Farrih's head jerked up. Beads of sweat stood out on her dainty muzzle. Both ears swiveled hard toward Hillari. The whites of the mare's eyes showed. The horse's desperation and fear was unmistakable.

Hillari paused in mid-motion. Her heart pounded in her ears. "Whoa, Farrih. Stand still, girl."

Their eyes locked. For a moment the world stood still and not a sound was heard. It was as if they were looking into the depths of each other's hearts. The mare heaved a big sigh and blinked her long, black eyelashes. Muscles throughout her body relaxed.

Laurie's voice drifted in from the trail. "Wow, she really trusts you."

Hillari slithered backward, uncoiling the ropes as she went. Once on the trail she handed Laurie the rope attached to the mare's saddle. They would use Laurie's buckskin like a tractor to help Farrih get some traction.

Laurie immediately dallied a loop around her saddle horn.

Hillari kept the rope attached to Farrih's head. She stood away from the gelding but close to the mare, not wanting to get the ropes tangled. Hillari took a deep breath and signaled to Laurie.

The buckskin was a cow-savvy horse and used to being used for roping. Laurie gently squeezed her legs, asking him to move ahead at a gentle angle while staying on the trail. In slow motion, her gelding eased forward, drawing the rope taut.

Farrih felt the tension and her head swung up. Her gaze darted side-to-side.

The buckskin set his feet, buckled down, and slowly moved forward.

Hillari chewed on her lip. *Is this going to work?* She gently pulled the rope tied around the mare's neck. "C'mon, girl. Give it a try."

The mare lunged forward.

The gelding moved quickly, keeping the tension steady on the rope. The mare rested for a second.

When Laurie urged her horse to move again, the buckskin slowly chugged ahead and the rope pulled even tighter on the mare's saddle.

At the same time, Hillari wiggled the rope and urged, "C'mon, girl! Tch…tch…tch."

Farrih reared up as much as possible and threw her shoulders and legs forward.

The gelding continued to pull.

The mare continued to flail. Grunting, Farrih's body finally rocked forward, as if she were climbing stairs. Higher and higher she rose until she scrambled onto the hardpan. She stumbled as she caught her balance. Her body was coated with gray sand. Exhausted, she widened her stance to steady herself and dropped her head as she gasped for breath

Hillari bounded toward her. "That was great, Farrih!" She wrapped her arms around her horse's neck. She looked at Laurie. "You guys did great too!" Hillari's knees felt rubbery as she brushed the sand from around her mare's eyes and off her soft muzzle. She untied the rope around her neck, and then undid the rope tied to the saddle. Tears welled up in her eyes as she coiled the lariats. Because she'd heeded the wisdom of an old cowboy, they'd rescued Farrih!

Being prepared has everything to do with coming out on the winning side. Practice and preparation are the backbones of every endeavor, from football players to Olympic athletes, from parents to businesspeople. Even children in primary school practice for their Christmas concerts. It's easy to see that we need to be equipped to face everyday life. But how often do we prepare for the biggest battle that rages around us? It's the battle between good and evil, between God and the devil. It's the battle for our hearts, souls, and minds. Do we prepare spiritually with the same enthusiasm we do if we're practicing for sports? Is there a regimen of training we follow to build our faith? Do we start our day ready to defeat the enemy with spiritual force and gusto? The apostle

Paul gives us a key to being ready to tackle the daily war between good and evil:

> Be strong in the Lord and in his mighty power. Put on the full armor of God, so that you can take your stand against the devil's schemes. For our struggle is not against flesh and blood, but against the rulers, against the authorities, against the powers of this dark world and against the spiritual forces of evil in the heavenly realms (Ephesians 6:10-12).

Verses 13 through 19 go on to define what the armor of God is. I love envisioning myself wearing His armor. We don God's armor by investing time with Him and studying His Word (the Bible). Then we put His love, and mercy, and grace, and wisdom into practice every day.

Hillari and Laurie saved Farrih's life because they were prepared. We can come out winners too by tying the rope of God's Word to our hearts. This lariat will rescue us every time we ride through rough country. Let's savor that wisdom from the old, wiry cowboy: "A smart rider never rides through rough country without a good rope."

Lord, open my eyes to the battle that rages for my heart, soul, and mind. Give me a passion to dig my teeth into Your Word and put Your wisdom into practice each day. Amen.

· Thoughts to Ponder ·

Have you thought about the spiritual battle that is being waged over your heart, soul, and mind? What can you do to jump into battle fully prepared?

8

BE STILL

Silence

Rows of snowcapped peaks lined Montana's Flathead Valley. The September breeze whispered through the golden aspen leaves. I stood in the center of the 60-foot, metal, round pen with my hands hanging by my sides. A coiled lariat was in my right hand. Shaking my head in frustration, I watched my new black Tennessee walker mare fly around the rails like she was a raving lunatic. Dazzle's head was arched as she looked over the rail and away from me. Her hooves thundered over the soft ground, occasionally kicking up clods of dirt. I dropped my eyes and stared at the ground to "release" the pressure from her, but she kept charging full-speed ahead. *What happened?* I wondered. I'd ridden her before I'd purchased her a couple of days ago. She hadn't been anything like this.

The mare blasted like a rocket orbiting around me. I glanced at my watch. Noon. I had commitments this afternoon. After I finished in the round pen, I'd need to spiff up before I went to town. My schedule was so jam-packed between work, church, and volunteer activities that I barely had room to breathe. *How long is this going to take?* My goal was to shape the beginning of my relationship with Dazzle by establishing myself as her leader. I wanted to end her training session on a positive note, but she wouldn't even look at me! I frowned. *She's acting crazy. God, what should I do?*

I kicked the toe of my boot into the dirt. In my spirit I heard, "Stop her. She thinks she's running away from you. Work her at a walk." My eyebrows furrowed. I shrugged my shoulders. Raising my lariat, I extended it to the side and walked toward the rail. Dazzle galloped toward me with her head to the outside. As she got closer she slowed and turned her head. Her gaze was on me. I raised the lariat and stepped toward the rail, creating an imaginary fence with my arm.

Bracing all four feet, Dazzle skidded to a stop. Instantly she pivoted 180 degrees and gathered her haunches underneath her so she could take off in the other direction. But I moved quickly and blocked her path. After a couple failed attempts to escape, the mare stood facing the fence. Her sides heaved as she gasped for breath. I lowered my voice and said, "Good girl, Dazzle. Just stand there and be at peace." All the muscles in her body trembled.

She's more comfortable running full-out than standing in peace, I thought. *She's like me. I like to run at mach 10 too.* Then I justified my actions. *But that way I get more done.*

While I stood waiting for the mare's breathing to slow I heard God speak to my spirit. "Do you? That's when you run off and forget about Me." I groaned because I knew it was true. When I was pressed for time, my mind whirled with my to-do list. I'd never stop long enough to ask God what He was doing and to see how I could join up with His plans.

For the next hour I worked with Dazzle, teaching her to take one step then stop. Another step, another stop. One foot at a time she slowed and gradually relaxed. Before the lesson was over, she was calmly walking around the pen, keeping me in the center of her attention.

When I turned my mare loose for the day, I asked God what He had planned, and I focused my eyes on what He was doing.

While training Dazzle, God tossed a lariat over me. He reminded me of the wisdom in Psalm 46:10: "Be still, and know that I am God." It's my heart's desire to join up with Him, yet how can I do that if I act like Dazzle? How can I be part of the incredible things He has planned when I race through life looking over the rail toward the outside of my life instead of looking toward the center—my life in and with Him?

In this noisy world of blaring distractions, how do we focus our eyes and hearts on God? For me, every day has some battles, but I'm winning by doing some simple things. The first thing I do is start my day with God—even if it's only for a few minutes. I make sure that I'm by myself and somewhere quiet where all distractions are turned off as much as possible. These moments set the compass of my faith to guide the direction of my day. The second thing I do is fun. I put sticky notes around my home and in my day planner. The hot-pink, apple-green, and bright-yellow notes add a rainbow of color to my day and catch my gaze. Sometimes I scribble Scriptures on them or a simple reminder to check in with God. When I see them, they stop me in my tracks so that I am still and know that *He is God*.

Lord, show me creative ways to join up with You and Your
plan throughout my busy day. Amen.

· Thoughts to Ponder ·

Do you race through life like Dazzle galloped around the round pen? When you do this, is it hard to keep yourself focused on God? What are some fun things you can do to change that?

9

STUDLY

The Choice

Clumps of blooming wildflowers dotted the rolling pasture lands in the Cypress Hills of Saskatchewan, Canada. The cool evening air rustled the grass. Gray puffs of clouds drifted through the pale-blue sky. Ross and Claire rode their horses through the milk cow's field on the way to the pasture where the cattle were calving. The married couple had ranched for decades, and they often rode together to check on the cows. It made the work go much faster, and it was a pleasant time to catch up with each other.

As they approached the metal gate, Claire reined her tall, black gelding named Sheik to the side. Ross nudged Studly, his sorrel stallion with four white feet, next to the gate. He'd installed a spring-loaded vertical handle on the gate so he could open it easily from the saddle. Ross's saddle creaked as he leaned forward, grasped the gate handle, and pulled.

Claire squeezed her legs, urging Sheik to walk through the opening. As they passed Studly, she heard a strange noise. A low, dull sound. She cocked her head and tried to locate where it was coming from. It resembled the sound of bone grating on bone. Instantly her gelding sped up and squirted through the gate. The noise stopped. Claire frowned. *Did that sound come from Studly?* After Ross had closed the gate, she reined her black horse next to the stallion. The hollow grating noise started once again. Instantly her gelding scooted to the side. Claire glanced over her shoulder. Studly's jaw was sawing from left to right. He was grinding his teeth! Although Studly wasn't biting, squealing, or being outwardly aggressive, he was seething. In the core of his being he was a stallion. His nature demanded that he protect his territory from outside intruders. The stud looked at Sheik as a male rival. Although the stallion had been trained to behave and obey outwardly, his heart hadn't been tamed. He was a stallion through and through.

A while back I was in a situation where I acted like Studly. I felt like I was a guinea pig in a mad scientist's experiment. My patience wore thin and I complained, but things only got worse. Every time I was around the mad scientist, my heart would pound. I could feel the tension rise up inside me. Frustration and anger became my close friends. I invested every thought into nurturing the bitterness in my heart. Then early one morning God arrested me as I sat in my prayer chair reading Proverbs 4:23: "Above all else, guard your heart, for everything you do flows from it." God spoke to my spirit with His still small voice. He said that the anger, frustration, bitterness, and resentment had built a wall between Him and me. This barrier was undermining my faith. Then God said, "Your feelings are *your choice*."

I felt like I'd been slapped. Of course He was right. By dwelling on those feelings, I'd caused them to grow. It was as if I'd been grinding my teeth like Studly. On the outside I behaved, but on the inside I was seething. God created people on a higher level than animals. We humans can *choose* how we will respond, how we will approach various situations. We aren't trapped in animalistic thoughts or behaviors.

In my situation, the real problem wasn't the mad scientist. Nobody could *make* me feel angry, resentful, or bitter. It was *my choice* how I responded. I'd programmed my heart with a diet of trash. As the adage says, "Garbage in, Garbage out." At any point in time I could choose to stop my internal tirade.

I slumped in my chair as I asked God to forgive me and to help me tame my heart. The transformation didn't happen overnight. I consciously had to look at the problem as if it were a red-hot, cast-iron skillet. Each time the situation arose, I could choose to pick up the thoughts, grind my teeth, and singe my relationship with God or I could leave it lie and nurture thoughts of how much my relationship with God means to me. The decision was mine.

*Lord, when I choose to harbor things that stand
between us, please tell me what they are and help me
overcome them. Amen.*

· Thoughts to Ponder ·

Are there any situations in your life where you are bitter, resentful, or angry? Do you realize those feelings build a wall between God and you? Have you asked Him to help you tame your heart?

10

UNLIKELY PROSPECT

A Dream in Disguise

The answering machine was beeping as Ute opened the back door and stepped into her home. She pushed the button and listened to the message. It was Beth, a college student and the owner of a 17-hands-tall thoroughbred mare. Ute had planned to buy the mare a few months ago, but the deal had fallen through. Between sobs, Beth was sharing that she was on spring break in Florida and one of her friends told her that someone at the barn, where she boarded the mare, had beaten the horse over the head with a shovel. Her friend had texted a picture of Tory with an enormous lump over her eye. Worse yet, the horse looked emaciated. Beth's voice floundered. She'd fallen behind in the boarding fees. The barn owner told her that Tory was only good for the meat market, and they were going to haul her off later that day. Beth pleaded, "I don't know what to do. Please call me back."

Ute's stomach felt like it was tied in knots. She'd discovered the horse the previous fall while browsing horse classifieds on the Web. She'd glimpsed a photo of a bay mare swimming in a lake with her rider. Upon calling the number, she learned that the owner was a college student who didn't have time to go to the barn. The mare had championship bloodlines and sounded exactly like what Ute was looking for. Her dream was to buy a mare and raise a colt from birth so that she could develop a special, lifelong bond with a horse.

When the sale price was discussed Ute had inhaled deeply. Perhaps the horse was worth the price, but it was way more than she could spend. Months later Beth called and lowered her price. It was still a stretch for Ute, but at least it was doable. Ute prayed about the situation, and she felt that this was to be her dream horse. After riding the mare, they'd struck a deal and set a delivery date. But the day before the horse was to be delivered, Beth called. The mare had contracted strangles (equine distemper), which was highly contagious. Ute couldn't risk bringing the mare to her barn and infecting her other horse. With a heavy heart, she cancelled the purchase.

Ute stared at the answering machine. *Could Tory still be my dream horse? God, what do You want me to do?* After praying and talking with her husband, Jay, Ute returned the call.

Beth's hands were tied; there wasn't anything she could do from Florida. She begged Ute, "Please take her. You can have her. But you have to get her today."

Ute rushed out to the garage and relayed the more detailed story to her husband.

Jay looked at her and grinned. "Well, find someone with a trailer and let's go get her."

When they arrived, Ute wasn't prepared for what she saw. Walking into the barn she had to choke back tears. Tory stood cross-tied in the concrete aisle, only a shadow of the horse she'd been a couple months before. Her head hung in dejection, her neck was sunk in, and every rib showed. A lump stuck out beneath her eyes. Worst of all, there wasn't any life in her eyes.

Carefully Ute loaded Tory into the trailer, and they drove her home. When they took her to the clinic, the vet confirmed the mare had a skull fracture that hadn't completely healed. Although they couldn't determine the cause, the consensus was some kind of blunt trauma.

Ute diligently worked at healing Tory's physical and emotional scars from being abused. Over the next few years, Ute nursed the mare through major health challenges. The hours she invested in caring for Tory created an indelibly deep bond between them. Whenever Ute would open the barn door, Tory would softly whinny and stick her head over the stall wall to look for her, impatiently waiting for Ute to come over and gently scratch her forehead. When Ute cleaned her stall, Tory would press her head against Ute's back or chest looking for attention. Ute's dream didn't look anything like she'd thought it would. In time she learned that Tory could never be bred due to a previous breech birth. To Ute, none of that mattered anymore. God obviously had had something else in mind.

· Tory ·

What dream have you had that took an unexpected turn? At times I think I've missed my dream because it didn't look anything like what I thought it would. But now when I look back I figure the dream turned out exactly as God had in mind. Sometime dreams come disguised in different-looking packages, wrapped with crazy paper, and adorned with ribbons that don't match. It's like the story of Moses' mother. Although her given name isn't mentioned in this particular passage, she plays a vital role in the history of the world.

When this Levite woman gave birth to Moses, an order by the Egyptian pharaoh was in effect. Afraid that the Hebrew slaves were too numerous and might turn against them, Pharaoh ordered that if a Hebrew boy were born, he was to be immediately killed. For three months after Moses was born, his mother, Jochebed, risked her life by hiding him (Exodus 6:20; 2:2).

Did Jochebed wonder, as she tucked her sweet baby out of sight, if her dream was really a nightmare? That perhaps the timing of her pregnancy was all wrong? Where was God in all of this turmoil? But she clung to hope and diligently kept her firstborn hidden. When she couldn't hide the growing baby anymore, she created a little boat out of a basket and placed him inside. Did she pray that God would protect him as she set it among the reeds along the shore of the river? Did her heart pound in her chest when she heard that Pharaoh's daughter had found him? Did she worry she might have the baby killed?

God had a plan! Pharaoh's daughter kept Moses and unknowingly hired Moses' mother to be a nursemaid. Moses was saved! He grew up as part of the family of the Egyptian pharaoh!

God's plan was carried out with His perfect timing. Moses was born at that exact moment in time so he could be prepared by God to deliver God's people—the Israelites—from bondage. Moses was a great leader, yet I'm sure that if we could go back in time and ask his mother about him, she'd say that her dream of keeping her son alive when all the Hebrew boys were being killed was an unlikely prospect. Yet she held on to her faith and diligently worked to see it through.

Through Ute's determination and diligence, she had achieved her dream too. One morning when she turned the horses out, they trotted through the dew-drenched grass and into the golden sunlight. Suddenly Tory turned around, walked back to Ute, and stopped in front of her. Towering over her owner, Tory's big brown eyes sparkled as she gently nudged Ute's shoulder as if to say "Thanks. I love you." Then she turned and trotted away. The bond Ute had always wanted to have with a horse had come about!

God works like that.

Lord, give me the wisdom and courage not to quit. Help me
persevere when You want me to. Amen.

· Thoughts to Ponder ·

What dream have you had that took an unexpected turn? Did you give up on it? Did you ask God what He wanted you to do? Is it something God still wants you to pursue?

11

THE TRAIN!

A Miracle

The Bitterroot Mountains of Montana rimmed the valley from north to south. The light June breeze and sunny days had melted the snow off the mountains' rugged faces and pine-studded shoulders. The snowmelt gushed into Como Lake Reservoir, which fed the irrigation ditches that wound through the ranchland in the valley below. So much snow had melted that the ditches nearly overflowed their banks. Many of them were so wide and deep they looked like rivers. Years before, railroad companies had built trestles to span them.

Lady, a five-year-old, blood-bay mare, easily walked alongside the railroad tracks. The gravel crunched underneath her hooves while 17-year-old Suzy relaxed in the saddle and reviewed her interview for a summer job. She hadn't been able to catch a ride to town in a car, but that wasn't a big deal. Earlier that morning she'd ridden Lady into town and tied her outside the local hamburger joint while she applied for a job. Often she'd ride her horse the five miles to town by going along the railroad tracks. In all the years she'd been doing this, she'd never seen a train. She wasn't worried about it anyway. If she heard a train coming, she could rein her horse onto one of the nearby country roads while the locomotive and cars chugged past. At least, that's what she figured.

Suzy's body swayed in the saddle as she rode around the bend and up to the trestle. She reined Lady to a stop in front of a gate. The fence ran horizontally from the trestle along the bank of the ditch to keep people out of the rushing water. She couldn't ride across the trestle because of the gaping holes between the railroad ties that made it impossible for a horse to walk across. Suzy usually led Lady through the gate and then rode her down the hill, through the water in the ditch, and then up the other side.

The water splashed against the beams of the trestle. The saddle groaned as Suzy dismounted. Holding the reins, she fumbled to open the gate. Suddenly Lady bolted as if she'd been stung by a bee. The reins zipped out of Suzy's hands. With her mouth open, she watched Lady spin around and take off. Hooves flung gravel as the horse launched into a gallop. Suzy screamed in horror as Lady turned and raced out on the railroad trestle. The sound of her hooves pounding against the ties ricocheted through the still air. Suddenly the mare lost her footing and crashed down. Her body slammed against the ties near the middle of the bridge and right over the ditch. The air was driven out of her lungs and she grunted. The trestle vibrated and then stopped.

Lady lay still.

Suzy scrambled onto the trestle. Her heart raced. Crouching down, she stroked the mare's coat. The bay horse's hide felt clammy.

Lady groaned. Her nostrils gaped open for air. Her neck and head were stretched in front of her. Her eyes squinted in pain, and her legs seemed splayed out like a spider's. One front leg was under her body, the other out in front of her. One hind leg was canted off to the side, and the other one was lodged between the ties all the way to the hip. Clearly she was in shock.

Suzy gasped and felt the blood drain from her face as she took in the details. *Oh no! What am I going to do? How can I get her off this trestle?*

She glanced around for help. The nearest houses weren't very close. Then she heard it. A train whistle. Tooooot! Toooooot! A train was probably crossing the side road beyond the bend in the tracks! Suzy couldn't believe it. *A train is coming!* Her head whipped around. She stared down the tracks. The train wasn't to the bend yet, and that was only 100 yards or so away. There was only one thing to do. She shoved herself up and sprinted between the rails toward the bend. Her red cowboy boots slammed against the gravel and the ties. She panted for breath. Pumping her arms, she ran faster and faster. *God, please help me!* she prayed. Although the train was still out of sight, Suzy could feel the ground shake from its rumble. Finally she reached the bend. She gasped for air as she spotted the train in the distance. The roar of the engine consumed her world. She ran down the center of the tracks waving her arms and screaming, "Stop! Stop! You've got to stop!"

Under her feet the ground quaked from the power of the train. *God, help them see me!* The locomotive, with car after car strung behind it, bore down on her. Suddenly she heard the hiss of the brakes. *They see me!* she thought with relief. The wheels squealed against the steel rails as they locked up, but the train kept charging forward. The noise was deafening. Suzy stepped off the tracks in shock and felt a rush of wind strike her as the cars sped past. She screamed, "Oh, God, please make the train stop!" A horrible realization assaulted her. She'd heard that sometimes it can take as much as a mile for a train to stop because of the weight of the cars and cargo. There wasn't a mile between the train and where Lady was trapped! Suzy took off running.

The metal wheels screeched, but the train was still sliding forward. It seemed like an eternity as Suzy hurried behind the train crying, "God, stop the train!" Yard after yard the momentum of weight and speed propelled the train forward, closer and closer to Lady still pinned in place on the trestle.

The wind swirled behind the train, kicking dust into Suzy's face. *Will it stop in time?* She ran as fast as she could, gritting her teeth as if bracing for a blow. The rail cars smashed against each other. Her heart constricted as she watched the train crawl closer and closer to the bridge. Suddenly the shrieking wheels came to a halt.

Suzy sobbed as she ran past the locomotive. Miraculously, it had stopped 10 feet from her mare. Lady was still so deeply in shock that she never moved a muscle when the train was bearing down on her. By the time Suzy got there, a small crowd of people had gathered around the heap of horse, including the engineer. Some were crouched down, evaluating the predicament and talking among themselves. Suzy knelt next to her mare.

The engineer stood over Suzy. "You're probably going to have to get a helicopter to put a sling under her to lift her up."

Tears streamed down Suzy's face. She stared at Lady, who looked so pitiful with her legs sprawled in grotesque angles. Her neck was stretched out, and her eyes had rolled back in her head. The worst position was the hind leg that disappeared between the ties. *Can Lady get it out with breaking it?* Suzy pleaded, *God, help me!*

A man who knelt next to the mare was examining her leg. He spoke up. "No, I think her leg is broken. You're probably going to have to put her down."

Everyone grew quiet. Only the train's engine chugging could be heard. Everyone looked at Suzy with compassion.

Suzy gasped in pain and sobbed. *So that's it? Lady is going to die.*

A loud moan broke the silence. Everyone's attention turned to Lady as another moan came out. With a sudden burst of energy, the mare shifted her weight. Everyone scattered as she gathered her legs and tensed her body. Suddenly she flipped onto her back. All four feet were in the air like a dog wanting a tummy rub. Lady rolled off the bridge and fell into the ditch below. *Splash!* The water sprayed into the air and seemed to swallow the horse.

Suzy scampered off the trestle and down to the ditch.

Lady bobbed to the surface. She struggled to get to shallow water. *Is one of her legs broken?* Suzy hit the water at a full run.

Lady found shallow water and stopped. Miraculously the mare was standing tall on all four legs.

Suzy waded across the creek and over to Lady. On the trestle everyone stood awestruck as the young woman wrapped her arms around the mare's neck. She rested her head on Lady's wet coat and sobbed. A few minutes passed before Suzy led Lady out of the water and checked her over. The young owner grimaced when she looked at the spots where the mare had lost some hide on her legs and stomach. Other than that, the bay appeared fine. Breathing a sigh of relief, Suzy turned and waved at everyone on the bridge. She yelled "Thank you!" before turning to lead the mare home.

Suzy will never forget that day—the day she totally depended on the all-powerful God who delivers His people. When Suzy cried out to Him for help, it was as if Psalm 91 played out before her eyes. "[The LORD says, 'The one who loves me,] will call on me, and I will answer

him; I will be with him in trouble, I will deliver him and honor him'"
(verse 15). It was nothing short of a miracle that the train stopped in
time. Even Lady's sudden burst of energy and motion seemed orchestrated by angels scooping her legs out from between the trestle ties and
flipping her on her back. One miracle after another played out in front
of Suzy and the people on the trestle.

In my many adventures working from horseback in the mountains
as a wilderness ranger and on crew for a backcountry trail-riding outfit, I've personally watched miracles unfold. I saw God deliver a mule
who was stuck upside down in a mountain "avalanche chute." When
I was left alone in the mountains to guard the food and supplies for a
trail ride, God protected me from grizzly bears. Another time a shear
wind (think "tornado in the mountains") struck the forest all around
me. Trees were uprooted and flung like toothpicks and everything was
destroyed—except my horse, my mule, my dog, and me! (You can read
these stories and more in my books *Horse Tales from Heaven* and *Heavenly Horse Sense.*)

Each time I witness the power of God, I'm amazed. But why should
I be? He's the all-powerful God who loves us and watches over us!

Lord, help me walk in the confidence of the truth
that You are my Deliverer. Amen.

• Thoughts to Ponder •

Do you believe in miracles? Has God delivered you or someone you
love from a tight spot? How did you feel afterward? Did you share what
He did with the people around you?

12

SADDLE BLANKET

Walking by Faith

A light, spring breeze and shafts of golden light drifted through the double doors at either end of the indoor arena. The place was silent except for the cooing of the pigeons in the rafters and the soft hoofbeats of two horses in the sand. Every day after school Cat, short for Catherine, and Holly met at a neighbor's arena to ride horses.

Sixteen-year-old Cat sat straight in the saddle and pressed her leg against the side of a liver-colored chestnut mare. The mare turned. Cat stroked the horse's neck and murmured, "Good girl, Delhi."

The last few months, for five days a week, Cat had been training the mare to respond to leg cues. A strange thought drifted through Cat's mind. *What would Delhi do if I climbed on without a bridle or saddle? Does she know the cues well enough?* Immediately Cat rode to the side of the arena. She dismounted, stripped off the saddle and bridle, and then scrambled back on Delhi. The horse now wore only a halter and lead rope, which hung limply over her neck.

Cat settled onto the mare's sweaty back and gently grasped a fistful of blond mane. Her long legs dangled down the mare's sides. She leaned forward and squeezed her legs. She could feel the muscles in the mare's back ripple beneath her as the horse tentatively stepped forward. It was almost as if Delhi were asking, "Am I doing this right? You want me to move?" The teenager softly spoke words of encouragement and squeezed her legs again, urging the horse on. After a few hesitant steps, the mare confidently lengthened her stride, and Cat's body swayed rhythmically as they walked around the arena.

Concentrating on maintaining her body position, Cat pressed her left leg against the mare's side. Cautiously, Delhi turned right. Cat's heart leaped. *Yes!* She rubbed the mare's neck in reassurance.

After laps that included turning left and right, the horse's confidence surged and her response time to Cat's cues quickened.

The teenager beamed. Her training was paying off. Delhi was looking to her for leadership without the use of a bridle, with its bit, reins, and chin strap. Cat shifted her weight back, and the mare stopped. "You've got that down too! That-a-girl, Delhi!" Cat exclaimed.

As she stroked the mare's neck another crazy idea raced through her mind. *What would Delhi do if I took her sight away?* In the wild, horses are preyed upon by predators, and they rely on their sight and other senses to protect them from danger. *Will she follow the cues if I put a blanket over her head? Or will she freak out, bolt, and shake the blanket—and maybe me—off?* Cat knew this would be an ultimate test of trust.

Cat yelled to Holly, asking, "Will you please get me a clean saddle blanket?"

Holly disappeared into the tack room.

Cat's heart raced. With her legs, she loosely gripped the mare's sides so she wouldn't get thrown off in case the horse spooked.

Holly returned and held the blanket up to Cat.

Reaching down, Cat firmly grasped the multicolored blanket and held it off to the side for Delhi to inspect.

Turning her head and with her nostrils slightly flared, Delhi sniffed the blanket and then seemed to lose interest.

Cat exhaled. *So far, so good.* Draping the blanket over the horse's neck, Cat leaned forward and slowly pushed it up the mare's neck toward her head. Inch by inch the blanket slithered up the mare's neck as Cat offered soft words of encouragement. When it reached the horse's ears, Cat felt Delhi's back muscles tense. The mare raised her head more. Cat paused for a moment and held her breath. Grabbing either side of the blanket, she gently lifted it over the mare's head and let it settle. She grabbed a handful of blond mane and waited.

· Delhi and Cat ·

The mare stood frozen in place, every muscle as rigid as steel. Her breathing was faster and shallow.

The chirping of the birds in the rafters echoed through the arena. Minutes ticked past. Delhi slowly lowered her head to normal position, a sign she'd accepted the circumstances.

Cat gently rubbed the mare's neck before shifting her weight forward and nudging the horse with her legs.

Delhi lifted one front leg high, not sure if she needed to step over something. She swung it forward.

The teenager grinned. "Good girl, Delhi!" She squeezed her legs again.

With jerky movements, the mare lifted her legs like she was a high-stepping horse and swung them forward. Step-by-step she trudged around the arena, slowly turning left and right on cue.

With each response, Cat's respect for the horse deepened. When they completed the circuit, Cat pulled the blanket off the horse's head and slid off Delhi's back. Her heart soared as she wrapped her arms around the mare's neck and buried her face in the velveteen fur. Cat had achieved her dream in training. Delhi totally trusted her—even being willing to walk blindfolded. Delhi had moved forward in faith—faith in her trainer.

When Cat shared this special memory with me, my jaw dropped. It had never occurred to me to put a blanket over a horse's head to see if my training was effective and if the animal really trusted me.

I thought of how much this story resembles our relationship with God. Our foundation in Him is built by walking in faith. Paul wrote, "We walk by faith, not by sight" (2 Corinthians 5:7 NKJV). But in order to do that we need to develop a relationship with God that is filled with trust and confidence. Years ago I studied John 10:27: "My sheep listen to my voice; I know them, and they follow me." I yearned to recognize God's voice faster and more clearly. It seemed like the chattering distractions of this world boomed louder than His "still small voice" (1 Kings 19:11-12). Because I was hungry to learn, God gave me an opportunity that stretched my faith so much that I've never been the same.

At the time I was working for some airlines in Kalispell, Montana. It had been another slushy, dark day in March. I left work exhausted from handling 149 irate passengers whose flight had been cancelled. I unlocked the back door of my home and heard the phone ringing. When I answered, my sister's distressed voice recounted her troubles with her car, an older, red, Chevy Cavalier station wagon with dark-tinted windows and bumper stickers plastered all over the back end.

Julie's husband was in the army and stationed in South Korea for a year. The army had recently moved the family to a base in Olympia, Washington, and then sent him overseas. Julie hadn't had time to develop good friends there yet. Her voice shook as she told me she'd taken the car to the same garage quite a few times and spent well over $1000. That day she'd dumped another $200 into getting it fixed. And now it was running even worse. Her wavering voice asked, "What should I do?"

During my college years, I'd worked in a garage. I knew enough about cars and garages to know she was being fleeced. After giving her advice, I hung up. As I twisted my long, blond hair into a knot, God nudged my spirit. *Why don't you go help her? You have tomorrow off from work, and you can fly free with one of your airline passes.*

I glanced at the clock. The last flight for the day left in 20 minutes. I could make it if I left immediately. Fumbling for the phone, I dialed Julie. She didn't answer. I left a message and raced to the airport.

I didn't realize it, but this situation was set up by God. Over the next 24 hours He taught me one of the most precious lessons I've ever learned—how to walk by faith and not by sight.

Sleet pelted the airplane as it taxied into Sea-Tac (Seattle/Tacoma) airport. I called Julie again and still got no answer. From the airport I caught a shuttle to Olympia. During the hour-long commute I kept dialing and getting the answering machine. The driver kindly listened to my story, and he recommended an honest garage. At eleven that night, he dropped me off at a motel. All night I called, dozed, prayed, and called again. I prayed, "Lord, lead me to my sister. Keep her safe." By morning I had bloodshot eyes and felt terrible with no makeup with me and only rumpled, day-old clothes to wear.

God had dropped a blanket over my head.

At the motel counter, I brushed my bangs from my eyes and asked which bus to take to get to my sister's place.

The clerk pointed out the door. "That one."

A city bus idled at the curb. Nodding, I rushed out the door. Instantly I felt God arresting my spirit. "No! Not that one."

I stopped. *But that one goes to her apartment, Lord,* I countered silently.

"Not that one," was what I heard again in my spirit.

I glanced at my watch. Eight o'clock. Time was fleeting. I had to find Julie, get her car fixed, take the hour-long shuttle ride back to Sea-Tac Airport, and fly home that night because I had to be at work in the morning.

Suddenly God's voice boomed in my spirit. "Go to your room, and wait on Me."

I climbed the stairs to my room and flopped down on the bed. I prayed and waited. An hour later, I felt God nudge me: "Now." I looked out the window. Sure enough there was a bus, but it was going the wrong direction. I took a deep breath and ran down the stairs. Climbing aboard, I paid the fare and sank into the front seat. The bus wound through downtown Olympia on the opposite side of town from Julie's home. Sleepily I watched businesses flash past. Nothing was open this early. The bus ground to a stop at a red traffic light. I glanced out the window into a mall parking lot. I blinked. It was empty except for one car—an older, red, Chevy Cavalier station wagon with tinted windows and bumper stickers plastered all over the back end.

Julie's car! The light turned green. The bus accelerated and turned the corner. I screamed at the driver to stop. Stammering, I explained why I needed to get off.

He nodded and amazingly turned the bus around and drove back. Parking next to her car, he opened the doors and wished me well.

I skipped down the steps. The car was empty. *Okay, God, what now?* I asked. Then I scribbled a note to Julie. "I'm in Olympia. Don't leave without me. Love, Sis." Tucking it under the windshield wiper, I glanced at the long building. The businesses appeared to be closed, but I felt drawn to one particular entrance. I walked over, grasped the cold, metal door handle, and pulled. The door opened. Stepping through, I looked down the long hallway of a strip mall. All the gates were down, except one. Woolworths was open. My footsteps echoed down the hall. I peeked in and saw the food counter. Julie sat at a booth, her back to me, eating bacon and eggs.

I walked in and tapped her on the shoulder. She turned, screamed with delight, and grabbed me in a big hug. With tears rolling down her cheeks she exclaimed, "I was praying that God would send you!"

Julie explained that she'd gone over to a new friend's home to spend the night, which is why she hadn't gotten my messages. But we were together now.

The rest of the day was a whirlwind as we went to the garage, and I helped her get all her repair money refunded. We drove the car to the new place that had been recommended. They fixed the car right. I barely had enough time to get back to the motel, catch the shuttle to the airport, and then board the last flight headed home.

That night as I sat on the plane watching the twinkling lights below, I savored the miracle God had orchestrated. He'd given me an opportunity to grow my faith! Only God could have led me to Julie on such a direct route. Although the situation had been about Julie's car breaking down, the crux of the experience was God taking me to the next level of faith. It was as if He'd stripped a saddle and bridle off me and then nudged me to go to Olympia even though Julie didn't answer her phone. When I'd landed in Seattle, it was as if He tossed a blanket over my head and said, "Trust Me. I'll show you something really cool. I know where your sister is and I'll show you."

Since that day, when I find myself in the dark about what to do, I remember that time. I stop, pray, and listen. I have the utmost confidence that God will always whisper the answer I need. All I have to do is follow His cues.

Lord, when I face the uncertainties of life, give me the
courage to walk by faith in You. Amen.

• Thoughts to Ponder •

Have you felt like someone tossed a blanket over your head and asked you to take a step forward? If so, what did you do? Have you thought of those situations as great opportunities to grow your faith? How might you respond more positively next time?

13

SCARED TO DEATH

Conquering Fear

Lou, a 63-year-old riding student, sat stiffly in the saddle. Although he'd been taking lessons for months, fear gripped him and he couldn't relax his 6-foot, 220-pound body. With every step, dust filtered into the air and the cool, early-morning breeze carried it through the indoor arena. The clops of a brown-and-white paint gelding walking in a circle around Kathy, the horse trainer and riding instructor, were the loudest sounds.

Kathy ran her hand through her dark-brown hair and wondered how she could help Lou. "You've got to do something other than walk, Lou," she encouraged.

The man gripped the reins tighter. Gritting his teeth he growled, "I'll do it when I'm good and ready." Silently he wondered if he were insane for doing this. He had battled the fear of horses his whole life. His resume of horse experiences read like a horror story.

At five years old he was thrown by his uncle's horse, got a concussion, went into a coma, and was hospitalized for two days.

A couple years later, his tomboy cousin pointed to a spot in the corral. "Stand right there. Don't be afraid. Stand still," she commanded. The next thing Lou knew his cousin whooped and hollered while herding several draft horses at full gallop toward him. Blood drained out of his face. Hooves thundered and the ground shook. The beasts towered over him. At the last moment, they swerved around him.

And the list could go on and on. *Every time I'm around horses, something bad happens,* Lou decided. The saddle creaked as he continued to walk Jag. Lou's chest tightened at the thought of doing anything else.

The crazy part was that he wasn't a cowardly person. He'd grown up in Stockton, California, which at that time had the dubious distinction of being one of the toughest little towns in America. He'd served in law enforcement and confronted dangerous suspects under dire circumstances. He wasn't afraid of any two-legged animal; he'd go down a dark alley after anyone. But when two more legs and a thousand pounds were added, fear suffocated him.

Lou's desire to conquer his fear of riding surfaced when his doctor spotted something wrong in his blood tests. A week later the physician told him the chances of surviving the illness were low. Lou's condition was stabilized, but during that time his mother and sister passed away and his brother had been diagnosed with cancer. Spurred on by thoughts of dying, Lou's mind had drifted to his unfulfilled dreams. As a child he'd wanted to be a cowboy. He proudly wore cap guns. Roy Rogers and Gene Autry were his heroes. He dreamed of riding. For the first time he realized that his fear of horses had kept him from pursuing his dream. A short time later the phone rang. It was his granddaughters' excited voices telling him that they were taking horseback riding lessons. Lou's mind brightened with the idea that he'd like to surprise them by riding alongside them. It was time to face his fear. So he set his goal, searched out a horse trainer, and took action.

Lou's confidence had melted the first time Kathy handed him a halter and told him to go through the stall and into the paddock to catch a tall, brown-and-white horse. His brows had furrowed. "Alone?" Kathy had nodded. Lou's heart pounded as he walked through the stall and heard the click of the door closing behind him. It reminded him of when he was a police officer and went into a jail cell with prisoners for the first time. The cell door closing behind him hadn't been pleasant then either. He broke out in a cold sweat.

Entering the paddock, he saw the horse. In his mind, the beast seemed to be equivalent to a wild gorilla he'd have to fight bare-handed. He approached the paint, but the mellow horse walked away from him. Lou knew Kathy wasn't going to rescue him. He finally managed to toss a lead rope over the horse's neck and bumbled through the haltering process.

A few days later Lou was standing next to the tall horse. The man's knees were nearly knocking together.

"Lou, this is a very gentle horse," Kathy assured him. "You'll be okay."

The war in Lou's mind raged. *What are you doing! You're acting crazy! You're over 60 years old! Why tackle this at all?* Then he took a deep breath. *I can do this!* A familiar saying raced through his mind: *The coward and the hero are both the same. They both sense fear. The difference between them is simple. The coward doesn't face that fear. He walks away. The hero faces his fear and moves forward.*

Stepping into the stirrup, Lou swung his leg over. The saddle groaned as he settled in. Even though Jag stood completely still, Lou felt like he was going to fall off any minute. On cue, Jag stepped forward. Lou wobbled and hung on.

For the next six months, Lou's mind argued continually. *What are you doing? Roy Rogers and Gene Autry are gone. They don't have cowboys on TV anymore.* Then he'd reassure himself. *You're going to be okay. What is the worst thing that could happen? I could die—but I'm dying anyway.*

Lou's dream prevailed. Diligently he showed up at the barn for lessons. Through Kathy's careful guidance, Lou gradually relaxed while brushing Jag before the riding lessons. The horse begged to have the white star on his forehead rubbed, and he loved pilfering treats from Lou's shirt pockets. Lou started seeing the horse more as a big dog that wanted affection and needed to be guided.

As the months rolled past and Lou refused to do anything but walk when riding Jag, Kathy intensified training by laying out poles on the ground in different shapes. Lou learned how to guide Jag through zig-zags, side passes, and backing up. With each mastered maneuver, the man gained a little confidence.

A breakthrough came months later in an unexpected way. On a sunny fall day, Lou stood in the arena holding Jag's reins while waiting for Kathy as she finished instructing some riding students on how to cross a short wooden bridge. The snorts from the horses echoed through the arena as they sidestepped and refused to step onto the bridge.

As Lou watched, the months of small successes from Kathy's training suddenly came together in a burst of confidence. A competitive spirit rose up inside of him. *I know I can do that! I bet I can do it better than they can!* He stepped beside Jag and climbed into the saddle. Gathering the reins, he nudged Jag forward. Without asking Kathy, he guided the paint horse toward the bridge. Methodically the brown-and-white horse trudged up the wooden planks and then clopped down the other side. Lou's heart soared! He felt like he'd won a gold medal at the Olympics! The training had finally culminated and superseded his fear. He wasn't afraid of Jag or of Jag being out of control anymore. Lou had become a partner with the horse. The man had persevered in facing his fears until he came through on the other side.

Lou broke the bondage fear had on him by staring it in the face, creating a plan, taking action, and persevering. He achieved his dream! Kathy's new nickname for him is "Mario," as in Mario Andretti. Lou now rides Kathy's mare Fancy, a world champion western trail horse. Lou races around like she's a Corvette.

Although our fears may not be the same as Lou's, we all have them, especially when we're challenged to do extraordinary things, such as following the dreams God places in our hearts. Throughout the Bible, God commands us to "fear not." By trusting God as our active partner, we can stare fear in the face and say, "God is for us, so who can stand against us? We are more than conquerors through Jesus!" (Romans 8:31, 37). God will lay out a training plan for us and lead us along the path He wants us to travel.

When we keep God at our side and stare fear in the face through training, courage will well up inside us and snuff out fear.

Lord, teach me how to be strong and
courageous in You. Amen.

• Thoughts to Ponder •

Do you have a heart's desire that you've kept tucked away because of fear? What would courage look like regarding that dream? What plan can you formulate to help you overcome the fear and achieve your dream? What trusted family members or friends can you ask to help you succeed?

14

CALLIE'S CHALLENGE

Determination

The hot summer wind spun dust into the air. Hundreds of people and horses swarmed the gravel parking lot that surrounded the livestock auction. Callie smoothed her red T-shirt, brushed off her blue jeans, put her foot in the stirrup, and swung into the fancy show saddle. She grasped the lead rope of her other horse and rode toward the outdoor arena. She wanted to warm up both of the dun horses before the auction preview began.

Her thoughts swirled as she rode down the grassy hill. Her long-term goal was to train horses, and she'd invested years into training the two mares she'd be selling. One she'd raised from a baby. Glancing back at the mare she was leading, she wondered, *Am I doing the right thing?*

Over the summer, Callie had been working for a professional horse trainer and riding a three-year-old gelding the trainer had for sale. The sorrel-and-white paint was the most athletic horse she'd ever ridden. Because her next short-term goal was to learn to rope, she'd need an extremely agile and strong horse. This gelding appeared to be perfect. But with the expense of college in the fall and some looming medical bills, she knew there was only one way she could afford to buy the horse named "So What." She'd need to sell the two horses she currently owned—and get top dollar for them. She'd carefully prepared the mares by grooming them until they glistened, and she'd borrowed a fancy show saddle to help make the mares stand out. She even put her platinum-blond hair into pigtails because one of her friends said, "Maybe some guy will pay you more money because you look cute."

The sun rose high in the eastern Montana sky and beat down on Callie as she arrived at the outdoor arena. Horses whinnied; people chattered. The bleachers brimmed with folks, and some cowboys sat on the top rail of the corral fencing. She tied the mare she was leading to the rail and entered the arena on the other. She sat tall in the saddle, her pigtails bouncing, while her horse performed perfectly. Callie's eyes sparkled when she finished. She hoped the crowd had been watching and noticed how well the horse responded so they'd bid higher.

After swapping the saddle and bridle to the other mare, Callie led her through the gate. She gathered the reins and put her foot in the stirrup. The saddle creaked as she lifted up and started to swing over. Before her leg reached the other side, the mare dropped her head, hunched up in the middle, and threw herself into a bucking fit. The crowd stilled as the horse went wild, tossing Callie into the dirt like a rag doll. The mare stepped on Callie a few times during the rampage. As suddenly as the horse started, it stopped. Calmly she loped to the other side of the arena and stood still.

Humiliated Callie pushed herself to her feet. Sand and hay stuck to her pigtails. Dirt was ground into her jeans and shirt. She assured the

· Callie and So What ·

people who had rushed to her side that she was okay. As she hobbled across the arena, her back and legs ached. *Great,* she thought. *Now everyone is going to remember the woman in the red shirt who put on the rodeo act. How embarrassing! I've been riding that horse for four years, and she's never bucked. Who will want to buy her now?*

Although she hurt all over, Callie got back on and rode the horses for the formal preview. Both sold for fair prices, but instead of focusing on that, Callie's thoughts spiraled downward during the eight-hour drive home. Negative thoughts assaulted her, accusing her of being a rotten trainer and a lousy rider. *How can I train horses professionally if I can't even ride one I've trained for years?* she wondered. Maybe she wasn't cut out for this type of a life. Worse yet, she'd forgotten to bring registration papers for one of the horses, so the sale wouldn't be complete until she mailed them.

The following morning her phone rang. It was the trainer she'd been working with asking how everything went. Callie shared her disappointment.

The trainer said, "Well, come by tomorrow. You can ride So What."

Callie's countenance lifted, but the next day turned out to be another disaster. The trainer had tossed the fancy show saddle on So What, and Callie lunged him. He responded well, so she climbed aboard and rode him around the outdoor arena. She cued him to lope. The gelding changed gaits perfectly. Suddenly he dropped his head, hunched up in the middle, and bucked. Unprepared, Callie's body hammered the saddle. All her bruises and sore muscles screamed in pain. After a few hops, she lost a stirrup and fell out of the saddle. With a puff of dirt, she smacked the ground.

The trainer and Callie looked the equipment over carefully and determined something was uncomfortable on the saddle that caused both horses to buck. Even knowing that, Callie's confidence had been thoroughly shattered. She was done working with horses. Finished.

A few days later Callie sat on her bed going through boxes of old papers. She was looking for the one mare's registration so she could complete the sale. She dug through her old school assignments. The teachers had asked the students to write about subjects that interested them. Callie's papers had been about raising and training horses.

She stopped what she was doing and reminisced about her first horse, Little Bit. She was a short, fat, bay mare that really belonged to her dad. Little Bit was born about the same time as Callie, so they grew up together. By the time Callie was eight, she'd saved up enough money to buy a kid's saddle. She'd saddle Little Bit, and then climb on a stool to pull herself into the saddle. Once settled in, she would ride around the small pasture. When Little Bit decided she'd had enough, she would hop into the air, curl her body into a "C," and buck until Callie flew off and landed in a heap. The little girl's temper would flare! She'd grab the reins, stomp across the pasture, get Little Bit into position, and then use the stool to climb back on the horse. Time after time the mare dumped Callie. Every time she rode, she would be tossed three or four times. But Callie never gave up. She *always* got back on.

Getting back to work, Callie found the mare's registration and scooped the pile of school papers back into the box. Over the next couple of days she mulled over the persistence Little Bit had taught her. Callie knew God had indeed put horses inside her. It was time to put the lesson she'd learned from Little Bit into practice—to put the bucking behind her and get back on and ride.

Callie's challenge of choosing to quit or to persevere resembles our everyday lives. She had to give up two mares she loved in order to move forward toward her next dream. Then everything went haywire. When we get bucked off life, it hurts. We might blame ourselves, others, or even God. We get discouraged and want to quit. But none of those things carry us toward building the life of faith God desires for us.

Our God knows how tough life can be. That's why He encourages us through His Word. Hebrews 10:36 says, "You need to persevere so that when you have done the will of God, you will receive what he has promised." A happy and fulfilled life is achieved when we strengthen our spirits with the Word of God and then put our foot into the stirrup and get back on. And that is exactly what Callie did. She now owns and is training So What, the horse of her dreams.

Lord, when life bucks me off, remind me that You're here to
dust me off. With Your help I know I can put my foot back
into the stirrup and ride. Amen.

· Thoughts to Ponder ·

Has life bucked you off? What did you do? Are there dreams God wants you to pursue? What do you need to do to put your foot in the stirrup and ride toward His plan for you?

15

BLACKIE

Choosing Obedience

On the outskirts of Mobile, Alabama, the mid-afternoon sun beat down. The muggy air was still. A long row of saddled horses were tied to a hitching rail by the barn. Some stood with drooped heads as they took afternoon naps. Others switched their tails and occasionally stomped a foot to shoo away the flies. Ed glanced down the row of horses. It was June. School had let out, and one of Ed's friends had asked him to rent a horse and go riding with her.

A group of people milled around the horses, trying to figure out which mounts to ride. Ed's eyes stopped on an obsidian horse. There was a spark in his eye that cinched Ed's decision. The horse looked like a kindred spirit. Turning to the teenaged wrangler, Ed pointed at the black horse. "I want to ride this one."

The wrangler's eyebrows furrowed while sizing up Ed's gangly 140-pounds on a 6-foot-tall frame. "Have you ridden before?"

Ed nodded. He was 16 years old and in charge. He knew all about riding. After all, he'd been on a mule when he was 4 years old.

The wrangler cautioned, "Blackie is spirited."

That was the wrong thing to say. Now Ed wanted to ride that horse no matter what.

After getting the horses sorted out and everyone mounted, the riders guided their horses down a well-worn trail through a 10-acre pasture. Ed loosely held the reins that had been tied together so he couldn't drop one. He nudged Blackie into a faster walk to get next to his friend's horse. The horses ambled across a grassy meadow dotted with oak trees. When the trail wound down a small dip, Blackie's body tipped downhill. He stretched out his neck, pulling the reins so they hung loosely. Ed's hands and body were relaxed as he visited with his friend. The horses sloshed through a small ditch full of water and continued across the pasture.

Blackie's body tensed, and he clamped down on the bit. He turned his head and looked at Ed as if to say, "Okay! Here we go!" Rearing up and pivoting 180 degrees, the horse leaped into a gallop.

Ed fumbled as he grabbed the saddle horn and pulled back on the reins. Blackie's hooves hit the earth hard, and the teen's rear slammed into the saddle. A wave of pain shot through his spine. Desperately he hung on as Blackie's body flattened in an all-out run. The beast was headed for the barn. His churning hooves sounded like thunder as they quickly covered ground. Clods of dirt sprayed behind him.

The other kids stopped their horses to watch the show. Laughter and excited chatter rolled across the meadow.

Squinting into the wind, Ed clutched the saddle. His heart pounded in his ears. Then his eyes grew wide. The ditch! Although it was only two feet across, it looked like the Grand Canyon to Ed. Dropping the reins, he grabbed the saddle horn with both hands and hung on white-knuckled.

Without hesitating Blackie cleared the ditch with ease.

Ed's body slammed the saddle again when they landed. His teeth rattled. He gasped and looked up. The barn was next. Ed cringed as he imagined entering the building at this speed.

Suddenly Blackie locked his front legs and dropped his hindquarters, sliding to a stop.

Ed somersaulted over the horse's head. *Whop!* The teen hit the hard-packed dirt on his backside, knocking the wind out of him. He groaned. Fortunately the only thing that was seriously hurt was his ego.

Yep, Ed had picked a horse that mirrored him perfectly.

In Ed's senior year of high school, he lost interest in school. Although he sat in the various classrooms all year, he earned failing grades in nearly every subject. After his friends graduated, Ed left school and moved to Atlanta. He was racing his car through the streets about 25 miles an hour over the speed limit when the flashing lights of a police car appeared behind him. The fines printed on the reckless driving and speeding tickets were huge.

Ed was sure he could get the fines reduced by appearing in court. When he arrived, 20 or so people sat in the courtroom waiting for the bailiff to call their names. When Ed was summoned, he walked up to the judge's desk and entered his plea.

The judge sternly interrogated him. "Are you living at home with your parents?"

"No, I left home. I'm living with my grandparents."

The judge raised his eyebrows and tilted his head. "Do you have a job?"

"Yes, sir."

"Did you finish high school?"

Ed stammered that he'd dropped out of school…well, not really. He simply hadn't graduated.

The judge held his pen over the paper where he'd write down the judgment.

Ed's eyes grew large as the judge scribbled in the fine amount. He'd raised it so that it was more than three-and-a-half times Ed's weekly paycheck!

Leaning forward, the judge told Ed, "You've got three choices. Either pay the fine, have your license suspended for a year and spend 30 days in jail, or go back to school at night until you earn a high school equivalency diploma."

Ed's days of being in charge had taken him down a dark path that led to strict consequences. Wanting to do things his own way wasn't original with Ed. In fact, that attitude is what the fall of mankind was all about. In the beginning of time, God created a beautiful garden for Adam. God told him, "You are free to eat from any tree in the garden; but you *must not eat* from the tree of the knowledge of good and evil, for when you eat from it you will certainly die" (Genesis 2:16-17). Then God made Eve for Adam. And they lived in the Garden of Eden together.

Along came the wily serpent—Satan in disguise—who told Eve that eating the fruit wouldn't kill her, but "your eyes will be opened, and you will be like God, knowing good and evil" (Genesis 3:5). By eating the apple, Eve…and eventually Adam…believed they'd know if God was holding something back from them. They were rejecting what God said was best and choosing their own path. They wanted to grab the bit and go where *they* wanted to.

After Adam and Eve ate the forbidden fruit, their eyes were opened all right. But they didn't see what they wanted. They'd brought curses on themselves, every living creature on earth, and the earth itself. By their choices, Adam and Eve lost the blessing of living in a God-designed peaceful garden in a perfect world. I'm sure God's heart was broken when He had to follow through on consequences and drive Adam and Eve out of the garden.

Adam and Eve and Ed and Blackie didn't want anybody telling them what to do. They wanted to be the stars in their own show. Fortunately for Ed, he came face-to-face with a judge who had the wisdom and compassion to help him realize life could be pleasant or miserable—and it was Ed's choice which it would be.

Ed reared up and did a 180-degree pivot. Suddenly he started listening to his grandparents, going to church, and attending night school until he graduated with his GED. During one of those summers he volunteered at the stables, and Blackie remained his favorite horse.

In the following years, Ed married, went to work for his dad, and attended college. Thanks to a judge who took the time to set him on a better path, he chose to live a blessed life by building it on the foundation of faith and obedience to God.

Our heavenly Father is our ultimate Judge. He says, "I will instruct you and teach you in the way you should go; I will counsel you with my loving eye on you. Do not be like the horse or the mule, which have no understanding but must be controlled by bit and bridle or they will not come to you" (Psalm 32:8-9). God lovingly gives us free will to make our own choices even though He understands the struggles we face. You and I can choose to live miserably by ignoring God's counsel or we can live for Him and receive blessings by heeding His voice.

I choose God's way. What about you?

Lord, please rein me in when I try to chomp down on the bit and go my own direction. Guide me in the way You want me to go. Amen.

• Thoughts to Ponder •

How often have you raced off with the bit in your mouth? Because you can't see into the future and you don't have the capacity and power to see how everything is interconnected, you can't make the best decisions like God does. What areas of your life have you been trying to control? What would it be like if you gave the reins to God?

16

HARDTACK

Survival Food

The mid-morning sun cast its golden rays at an angle through the forest. It was quiet except for the soft footfalls of the horses' hooves on the pine needles and occasional squirrel chatter coming from the tops of the trees. Debbie and I reined in our horses, and my saddle creaked as I stepped to the ground. It was time for a break to stretch my legs. I was also hungry. To beat the heat, at the crack of dawn I'd loaded Sky-Song into the horse trailer and driven over to the trailhead to meet Debbie. To leave on time, I'd cut my morning routine about a third. I'd skimped on my morning Bible study, figuring I could catch up in the afternoon, and I'd barely allowed enough time to catch a quick bite to eat before I went out the door.

I loosely held the reins so SkySong could nibble some grass. Digging into my fanny pack, I found a sandwich bag filled with my favorite treat—my homemade version of hardtack. I'd gotten hooked on this old-fashioned "power bar" when I worked in the wilderness. Hardtack has been served to sailors and armies since the days of old because properly prepared and stored it doesn't squish and will keep forever. Primarily made of flour, water, and salt, it was inexpensive and baked until all the moisture was gone, making it as hard as rock. To eat it, men would boil it, soak it in coffee, or smash it with the butts of their rifles. The ones I make contain nuts, flour, dried fruit, and semi-sweet chocolate chips. Although firm, the biscuits won't break my teeth.

Debbie and I chatted as I dug out a hunk of my hardtack. I offered some to Debbie, but she wasn't hungry. Using my teeth, I broke off a bite. We talked about exploring some new country, and as I pointed to the faint outline of a trail that went through the trees and up the mountain, SkySong raised his head and his ears swiveled forward. His gaze zoned in on my piece of hardtack. His nostrils flared; his whiskers wiggled. Licking his lips, he stared at my treat. I laughed and said, "Chocolate chips are bad for horses." But SkySong didn't care what I said. He wanted to try a bite for himself. Digging into the Baggie, I pulled out another piece and put it on my hand. "Okay, but you won't like it."

With gentle lips, SkySong snatched it. With his tongue he shifted the morsel between his molars and crunched down. His eyes lit up! Slobber formed in the corners of his mouth. I shook my head in disbelief. "Okay, so you do like it. The rest is for Debbie and me!"

I glanced at Debbie. "Are you ready to go up the trail?"

She nodded, gathered her reins, put her foot in the stirrup, and slipped into the saddle.

SkySong watched me tuck the Baggie with the remaining pieces of hardtack into my fanny pack. I buckled the pack around my waist and decided to walk a bit before climbing in the saddle. I hadn't gone a dozen steps before I felt SkySong's breath on my back and then a tug on my fanny pack. I swung my arm behind me and swished the reins at him. He backed off a bit. Within a few yards I felt another tug on my fanny pack. I turned around. SkySong's gaze was zeroed in on the fanny pack. I laughed. "Oh, I get it. You want to nibble on hardtack all day long."

I'd had enough walking. The saddle groaned as I stepped into the stirrup, swung my leg over, and settled in. SkySong glanced back at me. I was sure his eyes were sad. As I nudged him forward an interesting thought drifted through my spirit. *You could nibble all day long on God's Word. It's great survival food.* My mind whirled. That is what faith is about—taking the Word of God and applying it throughout the day.

I could easily do that. All I needed to do was focus on one Bible verse during my study time and chew on it all day. Joshua 1:8 comes to mind: "Keep this Book of the Law always on your lips; meditate on it day and night, so that you may be careful to do everything written in it. Then you will be prosperous and successful."

SkySong's desire to nibble on the hardtack started a healthy habit for me. I now carry 3 x 5 fluorescent-colored index cards in my purse, my car, and nearly everywhere I go. The cards have Scripture verses written on them so I can chomp on God's Word all day. It is *the* survival food that builds faith! Why not try it this week?

Lord, thank You for giving me Your Word as nourishment to strengthen my faith in You. Amen.

· Thoughts to Ponder ·

What Bible verse will you meditate on today? Consider how you can apply the wisdom and principles to your day...and then do it. Have you ever made flash cards with Bible verses on them? Why not make a set of 20 or so to use this month?

· Rebecca's Hardtack ·

1½ c. whole-wheat flour	1½ c. white flour	1 c. water
½ c. vegetable oil	½ c. brown sugar	½ tsp. salt
1½ c. chopped nuts	2 Tbs. oat bran	

Optional
½ to 1 c. raisins
½ to 1 c. coconut
½ to 1 c. mini chocolate chips
½ to 1 c. whatever else sounds good to you

Thoroughly mix all ingredients in a mixer using a dough hook or by hand. Spread ½" thick on a greased jelly roll pan and cut into one inch squares *before* baking. Bake in 350 degree oven for 35 to 50 minutes until dried throughout. Store in the freezer.

17

FINGERPRINTS OF GOD

Surprise!

Gray clouds cloaked the sky, obscuring the tall Rocky Mountain peaks that rimmed Flathead Valley. The green Nissan truck bumped down the long driveway, past the main house of the large, horse-boarding facility, and stopped in the parking lot by the barn. A bay mare rested her head on the top rail of the pipe corral and watched. As Cindy turned the key off, she looked at the mare and gasped. She turned to her grown daughter who sat in the passenger's seat. Amy's delicate lips tightened as she stared at her mare. The spring rains had been falling the past couple of weeks, and each day the mud in the mare's corral had gotten deeper.

They hopped out of the truck and walked to the corral.

Cindy muttered, "Wow, this is worse than it looked from the truck."

The corral resembled a pig wallow. Black goo had swallowed Oakley's legs all the way to her knees. Cindy knew the mare's feet would rot if she didn't get on drier ground—and soon. The mare's pleading eyes followed them, almost as if she were saying, "I can't stand this! Get me out of here!" Amy knew that with the contours of the land in this area there wouldn't be a single dry spot. She gently stroked her mare's forehead and looked at her mom. In unison they said, "We have to get her out of here today." They made plans. Each went to their own home to begin the search for a new horse-boarding place.

A couple of years before, Cindy was delighted when Amy got the bay mare. It was her grown daughter's first horse. They both treasured their mother–daughter time when Amy would train Oakley and Cindy would hang out at the barn. All through Cindy's childhood, she'd only asked for two things—cowboy boots and a horse. Each Christmas she was disappointed. Her father had grown up on a cattle ranch in Ronan, Montana. He knew how much work animals were—and how expensive. When he left the ranch to work on the railroad, he didn't want to deal with livestock again. He put his nose to the grindstone and eked out a living for his wife and children.

Fortunately for Cindy, her grandparents still owned the ranch when she was a child. She spent summers there with her cousins. They rode horses and raced over the rolling hills and grassy fields. But there was one thing Cindy was missing—her very own buckskin horse.

After graduating, Cindy married her high school sweetheart. By the time she was 20, the cries of newborn twins echoed through the house. With barely two nickels to rub together for groceries, there definitely wasn't money for a horse. That dream faded into the sunset.

When Amy got her horse, Cindy's heart skipped a beat. She thought, "I can love on Oakley too." But now Oakley needed a new place to stay. Cindy prayed for guidance as she thumbed through the Yellow Pages. An ad for a ranch that offered horse boarding caught her eye. It sounded perfect. After calling and questioning the owners, she felt peace in her heart about the place. Then she called back and asked, "Would it be possible to move the horse in tonight?"

"Sure."

Cindy called Amy, and within the hour, Amy had driven over to Cindy's, and the two of them drove down a winding road to check out the new place. The truck tires crunched on gravel as they passed a little farmhouse and reached the barn. Large paddocks with lean-to shelters lay in spokes off the circular drive around an arena. Perfect! They moved Oakley that night.

The following day, Amy busied herself grooming Oakley while Cindy leaned against the pipe corral. She glanced around at the horses in their paddocks nibbling on new shoots of green grass. Suddenly she noticed a colt. He stood about 10 feet away all by himself in an enormous paddock. He was watching her.

Cindy's heart fluttered. *A baby! And he's a buckskin paint. Wow. He's a buffy cream with white patches. Look at that chocolate-colored mane and tail!* Cindy's eyes were glued on that colt as she strolled over. He arched his neck and pricked his ears forward. Cindy stood by the rail. The colt walked closer and stretched his nose toward her. She leaned forward. His warm breath caressed her face. Gently she blew air in his nose. "Hello, baby."

He cocked his head side to side and sniffed her.

An hour later, when Amy was ready to head home, Cindy was scratching the baby's belly.

By the end of the week, the baby recognized their truck. He'd race

· Cindy's Dream Horse ·

forward, bucking and kicking up and down the hill in his paddock, and then he'd wait at the gate. Amy would walk over to Oakley, and Cindy would dig an apple treat out of her jeans jacket for the baby. After gobbling treats, the colt would rest his head on Cindy's shoulder while she wrapped her arms around his neck. Burying her nose in his fur, she'd inhale his smell. It was almost like she was a kid again except living her dream this time. She cherished the special moments basking in the colt's unconditional love. Hour after hour, day after day, the summer passed.

Then one warm-but-overcast August day when Amy was done, she walked over to the baby's paddock. Cindy leaned against the pipe fence scratching the baby's belly. Amy asked, "Guess what?" She went on to share that the owner of the ranch had asked her if she knew of anyone who wanted the seven-month-old colt. The baby's owner would sell him for a dollar.

Cindy's heart pounded. *Oh, my! Can I really get this horse? I would love that. But what will Kim say?* She looked at Amy. "I'd better call your dad."

Cindy sat in the truck and dialed. "You know this baby colt down here?" She paused and swallowed.

Kim had come to the ranch to watch Amy ride. He'd fallen in love with the colt too. He'd petted him, talked to him, and fed him apple treats.

Cindy tried to contain her excitement. "Kim, the owner wants to give him away! Well, she'll sell him for a dollar. He needs a home. I think he's supposed to be my horse. Is that okay?"

Cindy hung up and turned to Amy. "He said go for it!" Cindy's heart soared as she went up to the ranch house, paid the dollar, and was handed the bill of sale. She could hardly believe it. *Here I am, 50 years old, and God gave me my dream! I have my horse!*

I remember when Cindy bought the colt for a dollar. She called me and nearly cried as she shared this miracle from God. I whooped and hollered, and then we laughed and talked about a great verse in the book of Psalms: "Take delight in the LORD, and he will give you the desires of your heart" (37:4). I wasn't shocked by this new addition to Cindy's family. She and her husband, Kim, had invested hundreds of hours teaching people—including me!—through Bible studies in their home. Cindy had invested her life in her family and into doing what God wanted her to do. This was the first time in her life when she could afford a horse and have time to enjoy one. God's timing was perfect!

Our voices grew louder and louder as we put the pieces together that revealed God's fingerprints. He had to make sure it rained enough that Oakley was up to her knees in mud in the corral so they'd move her. If Amy wouldn't have moved her horse, Cindy never would have met the colt. We chuckled as we imagined God sitting in heaven dictating the order: "More rain over here. Make sure it drains into this paddock." Then Cindy and Amy had to choose the right stable for Oakley. Could the angels have shone a glory beam of light on the ad in the Yellow Pages? And what owner wouldn't want such a beautiful, healthy colt? God had made the baby Cindy's dream colors too.

Although Cindy never expected to achieve that dream, God hadn't forgotten. He'd chosen the perfect fulfillment and had given it to her even though she was 50 years old. When we're doing what God wants us to do, God will bless us in unexpected ways. Let's keep looking for the fingerprints of God. We're never too old to live our dreams!

Lord, stir my heart. Help me remember the dreams of my youth and watch for Your blessings. Amen.

• Thoughts to Ponder •

Do you have any dreams you need to blow the dust off of because they've been buried in your heart so long? Perhaps now is a good time to sit on the porch with God and have a chat.

18

A BLESSING THAT SNOWBALLED

Sharing a Blessing

Voices in the call center echoed through the room, which was as large as a gymnasium. Employees of the local phone company sat in the cubicles recruiting new business and handling customer service issues. Cindy ended a call and grinned. All she could think about was the young horse God had supernaturally given her. She'd wanted cowboy boots and a horse for as long as she could remember. She'd grown up, married, and had children...but still no horse. When Cindy turned 50, the dream of owning her own horse was covered with cobwebs.

God unexpectedly blew off the dust and blessed her with a buckskin paint—the horse of her dreams—for only one dollar! Cindy still couldn't believe it. Now there was only one problem. She didn't have a clue what to name him. She leaned back in her chair and savored names in her mind. One of her coworkers leaned over from her cubicle and the two briefly chatted. The coworker mentioned how she'd heard about a 10-year-old girl who dreamed about going on a school trip to Washington, DC, but it would cost each child $300. To the little girl's family it might as well be a million dollars.

The girl's dream haunted Cindy. Between phone calls over the next couple of hours, her thoughts wandered. *What am I going to name my colt?...I'm so blessed that I got my dream horse. How can I help that little girl get her dream?* When the questions merged, she knew it was inspired by God.

Instant Messaging her coworkers, she shared the two situations and then explained her plan. "I'm going to hold a contest. We're going to name my horse and help a girl go on a field trip with her class. So message me your suggestions for a name along with any amount of money you're willing to donate to help the little girl. I'll draw the winning horse name out of a hat."

The contest was a big hit! Workers messaged names and donation amounts. Cindy's daughter mentioned the contest to the three-year-old girl she took care of. Excited about entering the horsey contest and helping the schoolgirl, the little girl told her mother about it. The mother agreed to chip in some money, and the girl chose the name "Tuk," pronounced "two" with a hard "k" sound at the end. It was how she spelled *tuque*, a Canadian word for hat. Cindy's daughter submitted the entry.

On the day of the drawing, Cindy compiled all the names on a sheet of paper, cut each one out, and folded it up. At 4:30, she went into the manager's office. Although Dan looked like an older version of a bruiser football player, he had a soft heart for kids. He poured the slivers of paper into his baseball cap. With his thickset hand he stirred them and then drew one.

Cindy leaned forward, trying to be patient while he slowly unfolded the paper.

In his deep voice he read, "Tuk!"

Cindy chuckled. God had given her the horse of her dreams, and now He'd guided the manager's hand and chosen the name too. He'd also helped them raise enough money to send the 10-year-old girl on the field trip to Washington, DC.

I marvel at this story because Cindy's blessing resembled a snowball rolling downhill, getting bigger and bigger—geometrically growing into blessings for everyone it touched. It exemplifies the power of Luke 6:38 perfectly: "Give, and it will be given to you. A good measure, pressed down, shaken together and running over, will be poured into your lap. For with the measure you use, it will be measured to you."

Cindy had practiced the art of giving for years, and then God blessed her with a horse. God had given her the idea to share her blessing by holding a naming contest. As a result, everyone at the office was blessed to be part of a meaningful gift to a schoolgirl. The three-year-old girl Cindy's daughter took care of was thrilled that the name she'd submitted was chosen. And, best of all, the schoolgirl's hope became a reality because God encouraged a bunch of people to join together to give a special gift.

This true story inspires me to keep on giving, especially after I've received a special blessing. I'm sure it does the same for you.

Lord, show me opportunities to share hope from the blessings You've given me. Amen.

• Thoughts to Ponder •

When you receive a gift, do you pause to consider how you can use your blessing to bless others? Think of the last gift you received. How could you make it snowball into a blessing for someone else too?

19

GOING HOME

Hope for the Hopeless

The June sun rose quickly from behind the rolling, pine-studded hills outside of Mead, Washington. A white, compact car bounced across the grassy field. Kathi's stomach churned as she drove past the horse-driving course dotted with orange construction cones. Parking next to a small, blue tent with an awning where she'd be working, she glanced over at her 34-year-old son. A few strands of his bleached-blond hair poked out from under his white baseball cap that he wore turned backward.

Kathi chose her words carefully. "Joe, you need to stay close to me."

Joe nodded.

Kathi nervously repeated, "Remember, just stay by me."

She was taking a risk. She'd never been a photographer at a high-end horse show. Her adventures in photography had blossomed after a local newspaper had published a photograph she'd taken of a horse. A few months later, the owner of a fjord horse farm called and asked if Kathi would be the photographer at the Combined Driving Event their farm was hosting. The event drew contestants from miles around. After saying yes, she asked if she could bring her son as one of her helpers. They'd met her son and knew he was talkative and a bit different. Yes, that was okay, he'd said.

Kathi had omitted one fact. Her son was mentally ill, having been diagnosed with bipolar paranoid schizophrenia. Parking the car, she nervously wondered, *Am I doing the right thing? This is an important, top-of-the-line event. Will Joe act appropriately? Or will my plans be crushed again?*

"Hopeless." That's what the world had labeled Joe. Even the doctors had said he would end up living on the street, in jail, or in a mental institution. Joe's life had been peppered with years of despair, suicide attempts, hospitalizations, and homelessness. But he had never been violent toward others. His personality toward his friends and family was like a big teddy bear. Joe was always giving hugs. Rather than expecting presents to be given to him on his birthdays, he celebrated by giving presents to his friends and family. He was polite. Often when he wanted to talk with someone he'd raise his hand and wait to be called on. He hadn't asked to be struck with this disease, and Kathi's heart grieved for him. She never thought she'd be the mother of a mentally ill child.

Over the years she'd hoped and prayed that Joe would be able to lead a fulfilling life. But so far most of his experiences were components of rejection and emotional pain. Society seemed to only have room for good-looking businesspeople who achieved goals. Not many people would accept a mentally challenged man. Yet Joe needed love and acceptance perhaps more than others did. His heart was as big as the state of Texas. She'd thought that perhaps he could help others. When she mentioned it to him, Joe had responded, "I don't have anything to offer."

Tears welled up in Kathi's eyes as she remembered the exchange. Maybe the world had given up on Joe, but she held on to a thin thread of hope that there was a seed of greatness in every person God created— no matter what difficulties he or she faced. After she'd been asked to be the photographer for the horse show, an idea clicked within her. Through the viewfinder on the camera, she'd chased away the feelings of hopelessness that had plagued her. Photography made her focus on the beauty of where she was. It helped her look outside of herself. Perhaps the same could be true for Joe.

Kathi and Joe got out of the car. The air seemed charged with electricity. This Combined Driving Event, sanctioned by the American Driving Society, was one of the main shows in the country. Row after row of horse trailers lined the meadow. Contestants brushed sleek horses. Folks unloaded wagons, buggies, and carriages from flatbed trucks and then polished off every speck of dust until the vehicles and leather shone in the morning sunlight. Kathi's nervousness grew as the horse competition got ready to start. After getting her equipment ready, Kathi and Joe sat in camp chairs under the blue tent awning on the sidelines of the driving course.

Tucking a dark strand of hair behind her ear, she pointed. "Joe, do you see the number on that cart?"

He nodded.

Kathi continued to instruct Joe that when each new team entered the course, he was to take a picture of the contestant's number on the cart so that Kathi could identify him or her later. She added that he could take any other photos he wanted as well. She told him that being able to identify the contestants would be very important when it came time to sort through the thousands of photos.

Throughout the next two days Joe excitedly captured the horses on film. Often he'd point and comment, "Look at the muscles! Look at how they're rippling. I've got to get a picture of that!" At one time Joe had been a body builder, so he could relate to the horses' power. He watched in awe as the teams of horses pulled wagons up hills, around bends, and through streams. The beauty and majesty of the animals trotting with their muscles bulging and their manes flowing thrilled him. He was drawn to the horses with an invisible bond.

At the end of the day, Kathi took Joe over to see the horses up close. They were strong and powerful, yet when he petted them he noted they were sensitive inside just like him.

While editing the 10,000 or so photos they had taken, Kathi was delighted when Joe threw his heart into this part of the project as well. He'd been blessed with extraordinary artistic talent, and photography gave him a place to focus it. He'd periodically lean over, gaze at a picture she was cropping and say, "Now, Mom, you've got to leave the horses a little room to go…Don't put them in the middle."

When Kathi showed the photos to the sponsors and contestants, everyone was pleased.

Around the horses Joe felt accepted. He was free to give them love. The horses didn't judge him, and they were responsive to him. The more Joe and Kathi hung around the horse crowd, the more the people got to know Joe. They accepted him too.

At the same time, Kathi found Joe reading his Bible more than ever. He peppered her with questions about surrendering more of his life to God. As he sought his Lord in a deeper way, God began to change him from the inside out.

When the next year's Combined Driving Event rolled around, Joe's photography had improved so much that Kathi asked him if he'd like to be one of her assistant photographers. He replied, "Yes! I feel useful and important." Although he didn't have an expensive camera or fancy lenses, he took thousands of photos. At the close of the show each day, he left the security of Kathi's side. Armed with his camera, he wandered through the horses and contestants, asking, "Can I take your picture? I want to remember you." Then he snapped away. When he saw the contestants unhitch the horses and then strain to push the wagons where they wanted them, he heaved his strength into helping. He was so totally absorbed with the horses, photography, and helping others that he forgot to be afraid.

· Joe and Strauss ·

After the event Joe stayed up all night editing photos. He burned them onto a CD, and in the morning he took them to his mom. His voice oozed with confidence. "I can't wait till you see these, Mom!"

They walked into the den and huddled in front of the computer.

Kathi was stunned at the beauty he'd captured. Joe stopped at one particular photo. He said, "It's got a golden cast to it." The angle of the
sunlight made the picture glow. Joe had taken the shot from standing
behind the horse's shoulder looking toward its nose. The horse, wearing
full harness, was traveling through a rolling meadow. Only the wooden
stays and spokes of a wheel showed that the horse was hitched to a cart.
Joe pointed and said, "This one I'm going to call 'Going Home.'"

Shocked, Kathi nodded. Joe had never named one of his pictures
before.

God had performed a miracle. Joe, a man the world had deemed
hopeless, had changed from someone who had been disconnected
from society to a person who freely wandered through crowds of
strangers asking, "Can I take your picture, please?" He was a man who
had thought he had nothing to give, but now he's blessed thousands of
people with his photographs. His pictures have been published in cal-
endars, on websites, and within newspapers. Armed with a simple camera, his mother's love, and his faith in God, Joe proved that the word
"hopeless" doesn't exist in God's vocabulary.

· "Going Home" ·

"Hopeless." Have you ever felt that way? Jesus specialized in being the Hope of the world. He walked past the throngs of people who looked like they "had their lives all together" and zeroed in on those struggling in their daily lives. He gave Himself to each person who sought Him with sincerity.

The act of giving, which includes serving others, reflects the very heart of God. When we give, we take our eyes off ourselves and focus on somebody else. We move from being self-centered to being "other centered." I've noticed that when I give, especially anonymously, or when I serve someone through a random act of kindness, my spirit soars. The act of giving provides a natural high to the giver with no negative side effects. The best part is that it enhances our self-image. We feel valuable.

Joe experienced the very same thing. The more he took his eyes off himself and focused on God and others, the happier and more fulfilled he became. People accepted and loved him in return. The solution Joe needed was the opposite of what the world teaches. The world says take care of yourself first, and if there's a crumb left over then you can share. But the secret to a happy life is a paradox. When we give, we don't lose anything. Instead we gain everything. God shares this key through the apostle Paul: "The Lord Jesus himself said: 'It is more blessed to give than to receive'" (Acts 20:35). Hope for the hopeless is achieved through giving. The ultimate is when we give ourselves to God. God will mold us into useful vessels, no matter how big our challenges seem.

About a month after the second Combined Driving Event they attended, the manager at Joe's apartment building called Kathi with the news that Joe had fallen in the street while getting his mail. The ambulance took him to the emergency room, where they checked him over and released him. Not long after that, blood clots settled in his lungs and in his legs. Then Joe moved to his heavenly home.

Although Kathi was devastated by the news, when she looks at the "Going Home" photo she often wonders if Joe had a premonition he was going home to heaven soon. He'd gained hope and freedom through surrendering himself to God and by serving others. His contributions were acknowledged the following year at the Combined

Driving Event in their program. Under the words "Gone but not for-gotten" was a picture of Joe.

*Lord, I'm so glad there's no such word in
Your vocabulary as "hopeless." Amen.*

· Thoughts to Ponder ·

Have you felt hopeless? Perhaps you lost your job, went through bankruptcy or divorce, or a close relative or friend died. Have you talked to God about your situation? Look around you. Does some-one need words of encouragement? Is there something you can do for someone?

20

THE NANNY

Attitude Is Everything

The last of the sun's rays rippled across the golden-brown grass in central Montana. Tall metal silos dotted the rolling hills. The fingers of a gentle-but-nippy November breeze brushed past Lisa, her husband, and her eight-year-old daughter, Katie. They rode their horses along a dirt road that wound through the hills below a sandstone bluff. They were returning home after visiting a friend.

It was Katie's first trail ride on Nanna, her two-year-old Norwegian Fjord Horse. Although Lisa had carefully planned the day, it wasn't turning out the way she'd wanted.

An afternoon upset had happened. Lisa's tall, gray gelding had gotten antsy and she'd reined him in. He'd pranced in place and then suddenly reared. For a moment it looked like he would tip over backward, but Lisa stood in her stirrups and leaned forward to rebalance him. He dropped to all fours, and they had continued riding home. Lisa was a very experienced rider and took it in stride, but the episode had upset Katie so much that her nerves stood on edge and her temper smoldered beneath the surface.

Katie's temper was legendary. From the womb, she had been a fighter. She was a strong-willed child who was tenacious about everything. For most of Katie's life, Lisa had been single and a working mom putting food on the table for her family. The lack of a strong father figure helped generate a powerful current of anger within Katie that frequently surged. In a flash Katie could transform from a loving child into an erupting volcano. Before she was four years old, she'd knocked the wind out of three boys and bloodied two noses. Lisa had spent hours in prayer—asking God to help repair Katie's broken heart and tame her temper.

When Katie turned seven, she took an interest in ponies. She even tucked away her birthday and Christmas money to save enough to buy one. Lisa knew a middle-aged pony would be safe and offer the unconditional love Katie needed. One evening after getting ready for bed, Katie went into her mom's bedroom as she usually did. Wearing her pajamas, she plopped down on the queen-sized bed with the green comforter.

Lisa sat next to her. "I want to talk with you about getting a pony." Katie's eyes twinkled. "Really?"

"Really. But I want you to buy it."

Katie's face grew serious. In her mind she added up all the money she'd saved. The total came to $36. "Okay. How?"

Lisa laid out the options. One was working off the payments.

Katie skipped off to bed that night. After investigating different breeds, Katie chose the Norwegian Fjord Horse. Lisa found a reputable breeder, but when she called and asked about a middle-aged, trained horse, there wasn't one available. The breeder asked if she'd be interested in a yearling. Lisa passed on it. But search as she did, she didn't find a single prospect. Lisa called the breeder back to ask if she knew of any other breeders.

The lady said, "No, but would you consider the yearling filly?" She went on to explain that the horse had a mischievous streak and perhaps it'd be a good match for a young girl. Lisa considered, checked the horse over carefully, and agreed to buy her.

After much discussion, Lisa arranged for Katie to make payments. She knew that a middle-aged pony would teach her daughter life skills, but she didn't have any idea that this young horse might do even more. The filly was about to change her daughter's life in ways she'd only dreamed about.

The sun dipped even with the horizon and cast a golden glow across the grassy field. Lisa's gray horse and her husband's black, ex-race horse jigged sideways and impatiently blew air through their nostrils that formed vapor in the cool night air. They were headed home and wanted to get there now. To them, Nanna was merely plodding along.

The short and round cream-colored horse seemed content to not speed up. The horse's crested, Mohawk-styled, black-and-white mane slowly swayed in rhythm with her feet. Although Nanna was now only two years old, she was wise beyond her years. Lisa was sure Nanna knew she had precious cargo on her back and was choosing to walk at a sensible speed.

Katie, seeing that she was lagging behind, squeezed her legs against Nanna's sides to encourage her to speed up. When that didn't work immediately, she got frustrated and kicked Nanna's sides. The more she thumped on the mare, the slower Nanna walked. Katie whined, "Come on!" She walloped the little horse's sides and yelled, "Mooommmmm, wait up!"

Lisa shook her head while she listened to the whole commotion. She knew Nanna was slowing down because of Katie's attitude. She hoped Katie would figure it out before her temper blew. Lisa turned in the saddle to encourage Katie. "Just relax and squeeze your legs. She'll speed up."

Frustrated beyond listening, Katie pumped her legs against her horse.

The clop-clop-clop-clop of Nanna's feet on the dirt road got slower and slower.

Katie burst into tears and wailed.

Instantly, Nanna turned right and walked out into a field. The patient little horse had suffered enough rib bashing.

Katie screamed at the top of her lungs. "Mom! Mooommm! She won't stop! I can't turn her. Mom!"

Lisa stifled a chuckle as she ignored Katie. Obviously, the little horse, in her sweet and calm manner, was making a point about Katie's behavior. Perhaps this was exactly what Katie needed.

The little horse chugged away from the other horses.

Katie howled, "Mom! She's leaving. She's going to take me out here. Mom, she won't go back!"

Lisa twisted in her saddle and looked at the round horse as it carried her out-of-control daughter toward the center of the field. Lisa yelled, "Quit screaming, Katie. You know how to steer her back."

Tears streamed down Katie's red face. Ear-splitting screams drifted across the prairie. "She's not listening! She's leaving. Mom... *Mooommm!*"

Lisa reined in her horse. "Katie, pull on the left rein. Come on! You can do this. You need to calm down."

Instead of calming down, Katie flew into a tirade. "Mom! She won't listen! Make her come back!" Katie yowled and bawled even harder.

Nanna ignored the girl having a temper tantrum on her back. The horse stopped and stood still, pointing the opposite direction of the way they'd been traveling.

Katie's voice scorched the field. Finally out of sheer frustration, she dropped the reins on Nanna's neck, threw her hands up, and screeched, "Fine!" Then she sighed and relaxed.

Peaceful stillness drifted through the dusky field. Nanna's ears swiveled forward. She turned, picked up her feet, and boogied back to the road next to the other horses like nothing had happened.

Lisa watched in amazement. God had answered her prayers in this little horse! She was acting like a nanny, showing Katie that people throwing tantrums need to be put in time-out until they can settle down. The wise, young horse taught Katie a principle found in God's Word: "Slowness to anger makes for deep understanding; a quick-tempered person stockpiles stupidity" (Proverbs 14:29 MSG).

The best part was that it wasn't Katie's mom or dad or a teacher who had illustrated this lesson. It was Katie's very own horse that she'd bought with her own money and who was her closest friend.

Katie never lost her temper with Nanna again. From that day forward, she learned to control her anger. On the day Nanna took charge, Katie discovered that her attitude makes a huge impact on how situations play out, and how she responds is her choice.

Lord, when I'm tempted to lose my temper, give me a gentle time-out and show me how You want me to respond. Help me act appropriately. Amen.

• Thoughts to Ponder •

Do you have a hard time controlling your temper and actions when you're upset? Proverbs 15 offers plenty of wisdom for handling emotions, including these two verses: "A gentle answer turns away wrath, but a harsh word stirs up anger" and "A hot-tempered person stirs up conflict, but the one who is patient calms a quarrel" (verses 1 and 18). You choose your attitude and behavior. In the future, what will help you respond more like Jesus would?

21

BLENDING IN

Being Accepted

The sun climbed out of bed and cast golden rays through the fields in eastern Montana. A pickup pulling a blue horse trailer rattled down the dirt road that led to the fairground's entrance, leaving behind a twirling plume of dust. Lisa carefully dodged the potholes and edged up to the locked chain-link gate. She and her daughter had arrived so early that they'd have to wait for the fairgrounds to open.

Nine-year-old Katie nervously fidgeted in the passenger's seat. It was the first time she'd be competing in equestrian events at a fair. She'd be riding her three-year-old horse named Nanna. It was Nanna's first show too. Katie's stomach twisted. She didn't know any of the kids because this was a neighboring ranch town, but she was sure all the other kids would know each other. They probably went to school together. She hoped she'd blend in so they wouldn't make fun of her.

Several pickups pulling horse trailers lined up behind them. When the chain-link gate was rolled to the side, Lisa pulled forward.

Katie looked around. The small-town fairgrounds didn't even have a barn. Instead there were two arenas. In the arena she'd be competing in, white bleachers lined one side and bucking chutes lined the other. The contestants would warm-up their horses in a smaller, dirt arena. A narrow alleyway connected the two.

Lisa parked her rig under an ancient cottonwood tree. A half dozen other trucks and trailers scattered under the trees and parked.

Katie hopped out of the truck and curiously watched the other kids unload their horses. The sun glimmered off the sleek coats of the tall bays and sorrels. Their manes and tails had been carefully trimmed. Most of the horses looked like quarter horses or thoroughbreds.

When it was time for Katie to unload Nanna, she hesitated. Nobody had a horse that looked anything like Nanna. Katie took a deep breath, walked into the horse trailer, and untied Nanna. The kids' eyes bugged out when Katie stepped out leading her short, round, cream-colored Norwegian Fjord Horse. Nanna's mane, white on the sides with a thick black stripe down the middle, stood up in a four-inch-long crest, the traditional fashion for a fjord. The kids gawked and twittered while Katie tied Nanna to the side of the trailer.

Katie was the outsider who had come into town with a breed of horse they'd never seen. And from Katie's view, things only got worse.

She tossed the English saddle pad on Nanna's back and then hefted the saddle up. While she tightened the girth, she glanced around. Her heart fluttered. Every other kid was tightening cinches on *western* saddles. Then she noticed they all wore cowboy hats. Katie stormed over to her mom. "Nobody else is wearing a helmet, Mom! Do I have to?"

Lisa glowered, letting Katie know there'd be no discussion on that topic.

After bridling Nanna, Katie's lip sagged. She buckled on her helmet and climbed into the saddle. With her mom walking by her side, she guided Nanna toward the warm-up arena. The other kids wouldn't quit staring at her...and Nanna. *Everything about me is different,* Katie thought. She wanted to hide. Tears rolled down her cheeks. Her eyebrows puckered. She choked back sobs and whispered to her mom, "They already hate me. Why can't I be like everybody else?"

Lisa's heart broke for her daughter. Throughout Katie's childhood the other kids had tormented her for being very candid and a bit overweight. Lisa knew Katie would have to overcome this battle at some point. *It might as well be now,* she thought. Compassionately but with gentle strength, she stopped and looked directly at Katie. "You've got to dry your eyes. You're going to make Nanna nervous. You two will do just fine."

But things didn't get better.

People were scattered throughout the bleachers and along the arena edge, leaning their elbows over the fence rails. When the emcee announced over the loudspeaker that the English Pleasure Class would be starting, Katie dried her eyes with her sleeve and rode into the ring. She looked around with dismay. She was the only contestant! Everybody's attention was on her. She wanted to crawl under a rock. The judge called for a walk. Katie squeezed her legs. Nanna's cream-colored body calmly stepped forward. Each foot sank deeply into the sand, causing the four-inch-long Mohawk of a mane to wobble from side to side.

When the judge asked for a trot, Nanna refused. Katie's face flushed. She squeezed her legs against Nanna's sides. Finally she kicked the mare. The nine-year-old girl's temper simmered. No matter what she did, Nanna ignored her. Katie glared toward her mom, who was standing by the wooden rail violently shaking her head and mouthing, "Don't lose your temper or Nanna will freeze up!"

The judge fidgeted in the center of the arena as if she wanted to move on but didn't know how to handle her lone contestant without embarrassing her.

Lisa waved her hand and called to the judge. "Excuse me! Is it okay if I give Katie a crop?" The judge nodded.

Katie bit her lip. She wanted to disappear into thin air. After taking the crop from her mom, Katie tapped Nanna into a trot, and they finished out the class. Afterward she walked Nanna up to the judge.

The judge looked at Katie and said softly, "You did really well. Honey, I totally understand. I have shire draft horses that are really hard to motivate sometimes too."

Katie's heart soared. Somebody understood and accepted her—and it was the judge! Those words gave Katie the hope and courage she needed. She held her head high as she rode out of the arena and reined Nanna close to the fence. From the saddle she watched the other competitors while waiting for her next class.

A teen boy and girl ambled up to her. They were curious about Nanna and asked questions about Norwegian Fjords.

Katie was shocked when they said, "You did a really good job" as they turned to leave. They admired her because she was different!

Throughout the afternoon, Katie met several nice people because she stood out instead of blending in. At the end of the day, she relaxed in the passenger seat and watched the scenery flash past the window. A smile beamed from her face as she reviewed her day. *It really is okay to be different!*

Katie learned a precious life lesson that day. Being herself may mean she isn't like anyone else, but that's perfectly okay. This is the way God created her.

I often marvel when I look at crowds of people and ponder the fact that God created each of us to be unique individuals. "Is he not your Father, your Creator, who made you and formed you?" (Deuteronomy 32:6). Never again in history will there be anyone like you and me. Each of us has our own individual fingerprints. DNA is the blueprint of our physical presence, and each combination is one of a kind. If God wanted us to blend in and not be noticed, He would have made us all the same. Instead, He gave us unique talents and abilities.

• Katie and Nanna •

Another insight Katie learned was that it takes courage to be different. She's put that to work in her favor. In the last four years she's gone on to show Nanna throughout Montana, bringing home 4 medals and 17 ribbons. She's made a lot of friends through her unique cream-colored horse with the black-and-white Mohawk. Best of all, her hope was renewed by understanding she doesn't have to blend in to be accepted because God created her to stand out in a crowd.

God, thank You for handcrafting me. Amen.

• Thoughts to Ponder •

Have you gone through seasons of your life when you wanted to blend in and not be noticed? Have you considered that God created you to stand out? What unique talents and abilities do you have that you can share with those around you?

22

A DREAM GONE AWRY

Dealing with Fear

The hot, muggy air in Georgia smothered Christi as she stood on the sidewalk. Tears dripped down her face as fear consumed her. Her feet and legs felt like they were filled with lead. She could barely shuffle forward. Sugar, a sorrel mare, whinnied. Christi cringed and her body shook. *How am I going to get through this?* she wondered. She looked at the barn. It was only 200 feet away, but it might as well have been 200 miles.

I can't do this, God! Christi prayed. Her husband was out of town on business again, so she had to do the barn chores. Her breath came in gasps. *I can't handle Sugar by myself. Lord, help me get through this.* Christi was fine with the other horses, but ever since she'd been badly hurt in the accident, she was scared to death of her saddle horse. It hadn't always been this way. Only months ago Sugar had been her best friend.

Some of Christi's most cherished childhood memories are of times spent with her horse, but that was a long time ago. Since then she'd dreamed of owning another. It wasn't until decades later, after she married, that she and her husband were able to buy a five-year-old gelding. Christi was thrilled to discover that the owner of the barn where they boarded him had several mares in foal. Her lifelong dream was to raise a horse from a baby. This would be perfect. She could share in the joy without having to buy one.

At least that's what she thought...until a little red filly was born. Christi immediately fell in love. By the time Sugar was three weeks old, she already belonged to Christi. The foal stayed with her mom until weaning time, of course. Many days Christi would go into the stall

with them. The mare would nonchalantly munch on her hay while
Christi sat on the wood shavings that covered rubber floor mats. Sugar
would prance over and smell her face, tickling Christi with her dainty
whiskers. The knobby-kneed filly would plop down next to her and
lay half her body in Christi's lap. The foal would roll her big brown
eyes and watch Christi as she stroked her very own horse's velveteen
fur. Hours later, when it was time to go home, Christi would have to
move the filly aside to get up. Christi had never experienced a relationship with an animal like she had with Sugar.

But all that changed.

Sugar had grown into a beautiful mare when Christi adopted a
golden retriever named Giddeon. She'd brought him down to the barn
so he could snuffle around while she cleaned stalls. With hay rake in
hand, she glanced up to see the neighbors stopping their car alongside the front fence where the horses were grazing. They stepped out
with their granddaughter to show her the horses. Christi set the rake
aside and waved. She exited the barn and walked through the tall grass
toward them completely forgetting about the dog.

When she was halfway to them, she saw Sugar swing up her head.
The mare's neck arched. Her ears pivoted forward as she stared in Christi's direction and snorted. Before Christi could figure out what was
happening, Giddeon flashed past her, running straight toward Sugar.

Panicked, Sugar swung her rear toward the dog and kicked. She
threw her weight forward and kicked a few more times before taking
off in panic mode. Bucking and kicking as she tried to get away from
the dog, Sugar ran straight toward Christi.

Realizing what was happening, Christi turned to run. She glanced
back just as Sugar thundered past. *Whack!* The mare's hind feet sent
Christi flying. She landed in a heap, and pain shot through her body.
She lay on the ground groaning. The neighbors rushed over to help.
They offered to call the paramedics or take her to the hospital, but she
declined. Catching her breath and making sure nothing was broken,
Christi finally stood up. The neighbors said they'd walk with her to the
house, but she assured them she was fine. As the friends headed back
to their car, Christi limped to the house.

She awoke the next morning with a black eye, a hematoma on her hip, and a sore wrist. She slowly got better—even the wrist she found out later she'd cracked when trying to break her fall.

Weeks later, when her body had healed, Christi returned to her routine…except a wave of fear would crash over her when she'd get near her horse. The feeling became so strong that she purposely distanced herself from Sugar. Christi asked her husband to take care of her.

Because she felt foolish about her reaction, Christi never told anyone what was going on. The fear became so overpowering that if she was near Sugar when the horse shook off dust or stomped a foot, Christi would scream and her heart would pound. As the months went by, she withheld her emotions so much that she no longer felt a bond with Sugar. She dreaded the times when her husband was out of town and she was responsible for all the chores.

Days like today.

Christi stood on the sidewalk trembling. Tears rolled down her cheeks. *How long is this going to go on, Lord? Please help me get through this. I can't do this anymore.* Twenty minutes later she managed to shuffle into the barn. One by one she haltered the horses and led them out to the pasture until only Sugar was left inside. Christi's mouth was dry and her body quaked as she stood next to the stall. Her heart pounded. She forced herself to slip into Sugar's stall and buckle the halter around her head. While leading the horse out of the barn, she held her breath and kept the mare as far away from her as possible. The whole time she was braced against a possible blow.

While cleaning the stalls, Christi's heart ached. She knew it wasn't fair to Sugar. The horse hadn't hurt her on purpose. *God, please help me get over this,* Christi prayed. When she was done with the work, she brought the horses back into the barn, cringing even as she managed to get Sugar into her stall. It took only minutes to retrace the steps to the house that had taken her 20 minutes to walk before.

Christi took a shower and then felt led to do an unusual thing for her. She went to her computer, sat down, and turned it on. Drawn to a website she'd never been on before, she read the words of an internationally famous horse trainer. The article explained that God chose certain people to be caretakers of His beloved creations. Horses were precious gifts from Him. People, as caretakers, are to have an understanding of the horses' actions and not be filled with fear. God never intended for His followers to be fearful.

The word "fearful" jumped out at Christi. Instantly tears streamed down her cheeks. Ever since the accident she'd nursed fear—the fear of getting physically hurt again. Fear had become all-consuming and debilitating. It cloaked her entire life. She was viewing Sugar through a dark veil of fear.

Christi wiped the tears from her cheeks with a tissue and reviewed the accident. Sugar wasn't mean. She was just scared, and her panicked attention had been focused on the dog. *She didn't kick me on purpose. She didn't intentionally hurt me.*

Christi took a deep breath. She knew God had led her to this article and shared His heart. He'd given Sugar to her as a gift. He wanted her to enjoy His precious creations, including the horse. The Holy Spirit poured a soothing balm of peace over her. She'd never experienced anything like that before. The chains of fear that bound her heart broke and fell away. There had been times in the past when she'd received guidance from God and worked through issues, but this was an instant and complete release from bondage!

• Sugar and Christi •

Christi felt so lighthearted that she got up and nearly skipped down the sidewalk. She walked to the barn and into Sugar's stall without any hesitation. Christi gently stroked her horse's forehead without fear. "Oh, Sugar, I love you so much."

With her deep-brown eyes, Sugar looked softly at Christi like nothing negative had happened. Then the mare stuck out her nose, asking for a kiss like she had her whole life. Overwhelming joy rose inside Christi. She kissed her horse, wrapped her arms around Sugar's neck, and laughed joyfully. God had supernaturally delivered her from the grip of fear!

Fear is a difficult emotion. One way to think about it is through an acronym. Have you heard of this concept? Fear is…

False
Evidence
Appearing
Real

Fear is usually nothing more than a response based on inaccurate feelings. The false evidence Christi believed was that Sugar was a mean horse who meant to hurt her. It destroyed their relationship.

One of the most amazing stories about fear's potential for destroying relationships revolves around the birth of Jesus Christ. In Matthew 1:18-24, we discover that a woman named Mary was pledged to marry a man named Joseph. Their families had agreed to the union. Back in those days, pledges were even stronger than getting engaged is today. The only way a pledge could be legally canceled was through sexual sin or death. The upcoming marriage was set in stone.

When Mary shared the news with Joseph that she was pregnant and that the baby was from God, Joseph didn't believe her. And it wasn't long before the scandalous news was out on the street. Mary was pregnant! That was a big deal. In fact, it was considered so heinous that according to the Jewish law of the time, Mary could legally be stoned to death.

Joseph knew he wasn't the father of the baby. Since he didn't believe Mary, I'm sure he wondered who the other man was. And how his beloved Mary could betray him and their pledge by being with someone else. Joseph and Mary had planned their lives together, and now this! False evidence appearing real consumed his thoughts. Joseph felt like he'd been kicked. In his mind the relationship was over…done… finished. Because Joseph still loved Mary, he decided to "take care of things quietly so Mary would not be disgraced" (Matthew 1:18-21 MSG).

Then one night an angel of God appeared to Joseph in a dream.

"Joseph son of David, do not be afraid to take Mary home as your wife, because what is conceived in her is from the Holy Spirit" (Matthew 1:20).

Did you catch that? The angel said "Do not be afraid."

When I read that passage, my mind translates it as "Joseph, this fear you have is 'false evidence appearing real.' It's blocking your good judgment and ripping apart your family. Fear separates and divides. It's causing you to step away from God's divine plan for your life. Snap to and get your thoughts back on Him. He'll take care of this situation for you."

Joseph received the words from the angel and was delivered from his fear. "He did what the angel of the Lord had commanded him and took Mary home as his wife" (Matthew 1:24).

Fear is a powerful force that can disguise itself in insidious ways. It throws up a facade and builds seemingly insurmountable barricades. It erodes our hopes of obtaining our dreams. Oftentimes we don't recognize fear until it has a firm grip on us just like it did on Christi and Joseph. Fear destroys relationships and makes us afraid to restore them or establish new ones.

The great news is that God is in the business of shining the light of truth on false evidence appearing real. He helps us conquer fear, restore our relationships, and build up our hope.

Lord, when fear first enters my mind, please reveal it to me so that I can instantly turn to You so we can kick it out together. Help me focus on You. Amen.

· Thoughts to Ponder ·

Has fear held you captive? Have you thought of it as "**F**alse **E**vidence **A**ppearing **R**eal"? How can that acronym help you handle fear from now on?

23

BOON AND THE BIRDS

Rebuilding

The sun glistened off the snowcapped Rocky Mountains that towered over the lush Bitterroot Valley in western Montana. In the lower elevations clumps of bright-yellow flowers dotted the hillsides. The cool May breeze rolled down the mountains and across the grassy pastures of the ranch. Mares were lying in the sun with their babies romping by their sides. Wendy was leading her two-year-old paint stallion across the ranch yard toward the breeding shed.

Boon arched his neck and pranced, his mostly black body shimmering in the sunlight. Only two patches of white hair were splashed on him—one on his neck and the other over his hip. His gaze darted about as he surveyed his surroundings. He was young, but he'd already filled out and looked like a stout, work-on-the-ranch, roping horse.

· Boon ·

Normally Wendy loved planning the babies within her herd of 50 head or so, but today an ominous cloud hung over her that she couldn't shake. Absorbed in her grief over the tragic events that had occurred lately, she wondered if she was on the right track.

More than 30 years ago, Wendy had scraped together every penny she had to purchase her first broodmare. The mare was older, but she produced some fine offspring. Wendy fought tooth and nail to work hard, save money, and eventually buy a ranch. Many nights she poured over pedigrees and planned strategic purchases of horses to fulfill the dream God had placed in her heart from the time she was a little girl. She wanted to make a significant contribution to the equine breeding world by improving genetics. Her horses had gained quite a bit of fame, and they'd been sold around the world. Some had become jumping horses competing in England, some were professional polo horses in Argentina, and there were breeding ranches in California and Australia that had snatched up several. Some of the working cattle ranches in Montana wanted the bloodlines she'd established.

Wendy had been living her dream—and then she hit a brick wall. This spring one of her fillies developed a rare disease. The baby went from a healthy, bounding filly to one that laid down on the stall floor and refused to get up. Around the clock Wendy had massaged its legs and doctored it. The filly would place her head in Wendy's lap, looking up at her with innocent, loving eyes. But the little girl deteriorated so much that Wendy had to put her down. Heartbroken, she cried until her eyes felt raw.

Shortly after that a bouncy, month-old colt bloated as if he were bleeding internally. Within hours he too had died. When one of her broodmares didn't come in for the morning feeding, Wendy went out into the pasture and found the mare's four-month-old filly pawing at her dead mom's side. Now Wendy had an orphaned filly to raise too. *The mare looked fine last night*, Wendy thought. The autopsy revealed that the horse had died of a huge, cancerous tumor that had closed off her intestines.

The three freak deaths so close together spun Wendy into depression. *I didn't get into the business to watch horses die*, reverberated through her mind.

The stallion's hooves clopped on the hard-packed dirt as they approached the breeding shed. Boon's head swung up and his ears pricked forward as they neared the wide doorway. He'd spotted a mare standing in the stall…or rather he smelled her. He gave a low nicker. The mare responded with a chortle. Wendy walked through the doorway coaching Boon to be quiet.

A pigeon was nesting on the sill above the barn door. The movement of the horse coming in scared the bird. It screeched and dive-bombed

Boon's head. The stallion spooked sideways. Wendy scrambled to stay out from under him and, at the same time, maintain control. After she calmed the stallion down, Wendy wanted to throw her hands in the air and scream. This was Boon's first breeding, and she wanted it to go smoothly. Horses, like all animals, learn and remember from their first experiences. She knew it was important to do everything right and keep everyone calm. This interruption in her well-laid plans blew the lid off any serenity she had left.

That night at dinner, Wendy growled to Gary, her husband, "Those stupid birds! I've got to get that nest down. This happens every spring!" In years past it had been tolerable because the horses were used to the birds. But Boon hadn't had a clue it was coming.

The next day Wendy grabbed a long rake and swept the pigeon nest off the ledge. Two whitish-tan, speckled eggs fell to the ground and broke. The little yolks sat on top of the straw. Wendy's eyebrows furrowed with sadness, but she consoled herself. *We have too many pigeons anyway. They mess up the hay.* But still, breaking the eggs and terminating the pigeons' babies added to the dark cloud above her head.

The next time she led Boon toward the barn he jigged when they got close. His gaze darted back and forth. Wendy tried to keep him calm…and then *Poof!* Two pigeons flew into his face. Wide-eyed, Boon spooked again.

The birds had rebuilt their nest above the doorway! Wendy was at her wit's end. *Will things ever right themselves?*

The war was on.

Wendy got the rake and destroyed the nest again.

The pigeons rebuilt.

She destroyed the nest again. This time another egg dropped to the ground and broke. The yolk stood still a moment before it dribbled away.

A couple of days later, Wendy ambled into the breeding shed to do chores. She noticed a pigeon flying into the barn from outside. It had a piece of straw in its beak. The bird looked like it was smiling. Wendy stood still, confounded. *This bird is not going to give up! She's going to keep rebuilding her nest no matter what. And she's happy about it.*

Compassion rose inside Wendy. *That bird deserves to have a nest. All she wants is a baby. Even though she lost all those other babies, she's going to keep trying because a baby is worth it. And I'm going to let her have it.* Wendy felt the Lord touch her heart with that message of encouragement. *Keep trying because babies are worth it.*

Wendy took the lesson to heart and meditated on it. Her new focus broke the bonds of depression that had clung to her. God's intervention set her free. Wendy had slipped into the depths of despair because it looked like her dream had been destroyed.

Another person who may have felt that was David. Before he became king of ancient Israel, he may have felt the way Wendy did when he led King Saul's army back to a town named Ziklag. They discovered the town had been destroyed in their absence, and all their families had been kidnapped. The men wanted to stone David because they were bitter in spirit.

What the mighty leader did next amazes me. "David encouraged himself in the Lord his God" (1 Samuel 30:6 kjv). When everyone and everything seemed against him—even his men wanted to kill him—David turned to God for encouragement and guidance. David asked whether he should pursue the raiders. God said yes, so David did. When his army came upon the Amalekites, the Israelites slew almost everyone, rescued the kidnapped people, and gained the spoils the raiders had been amassing.

When Wendy encouraged herself with words from God, she grabbed hold of victory too. The key is to meditate on God's Word and do what He says. He will fill us with hope and see us through our circumstances.

Are you wondering about Boon and the birds? During the days the nest was down, Wendy worked Boon through his skittishness. She never knocked down any more nests, and the pigeons settled in and hatched two babies.

This past winter I met with Wendy at the ranch and asked her to show me around. As we walked through the wide doorway of the breeding shed, four pigeons dive-bombed us. I nearly jumped out of my skin. Wendy laughed so hard her whole body shook. She said those pigeons are great reminders of the wisdom she got from God: "When things look overwhelming, keep on and don't stop. When you get to the other side, it's all worth it."

Lord, when I'm down and blue, please give me
words of encouragement—special ones from
Your heart to mine. Amen.

· Thoughts to Ponder ·

Do you get depressed when it seems like life is stacked against you? Like there's no way you can come out ahead? What options do you have when that feeling comes?

24

THE FLOOD!

Praying for a Miracle

Tuesday, October 20, 1998, Gonzales, Texas

Robin's fingers gripped the cold bathroom sink. Her heart pounded as her eyes rested on the words she'd written on the mirror: "God can work miracles." She swallowed and focused on the rest. "With hope in our lives, all else is possible." She closed her eyes. *God, thank You for protecting my family and friends. Now what about the horses?*

The past few days had been a raging nightmare. Storm systems had collided. One contained the residual moisture from the tropical cyclone Madeline. With the 22 inches of torrential rain that had fallen over the weekend, the Guadalupe River, which normally flowed along the west side of downtown Gonzales, had been transformed into a deadly flash flood. The river had crested at 51 feet—flood stage was 31 feet. The "100-year flood" swept through portions of the city and surrounding countryside. Many roads had been barricaded for days. Media reports were constantly providing updates on deaths and devastation.

Although Robin's home was on a hill above downtown and wasn't in danger of flooding, emotionally she was exhausted from praying nonstop for family and friends who potentially were in danger…and for her horses.

As she looked in the mirror, a memory surged through her mind. A few days before, she'd walked down to the park a half mile away. The closer she got to the river, the louder the roar of the water until it was deafening. When she got to the riverbank, all she could see for miles was dirty brown water sweeping away trees and cars. On a little island in the river and on the far bank, soaking-wet cows stood with their heads hanging low, exhausted from being swept down the river until they managed to clamber up the banks to safety. Other cows thrashed as they still floated down the river, their mournful moos piercing the air. She watched as the current swept a cow off its feet. It bobbed downstream trying to hold its head above water. She shuddered as she thought about her horses. *Are they alive? Did they get swept away like that cow?*

Robin's horses were pastured on a ranch 17 miles from town. She had no way of knowing if they were okay. There wasn't anybody who lived on the land or close by that she could contact, and the roads going out there had been under water. A creek ran through the pasture, dividing it in two. The barn was on higher ground, and if the horses were up by the barn, they might be okay. But if they'd been on the other side of the creek when the flash flood hit…

Robin shook her head. She especially couldn't bear to think of her horse Gus being washed into the raging creek where he'd drown or be battered by trees and debris until he was killed. *Is Gus okay? God, I know You can save and protect him. I know You love horses. Please help them.* But deep inside there was a little doubt that was tearing her heart. Would God do this for her? Was she worth that kind of miracle?

As a caseworker for Child Protective Services, all day long Robin was battered emotionally while she acted as an advocate for abused and neglected children. The system seemed inadequate in a lot of cases. Often nothing changed for the children. At those times she wondered if her work mattered. And when she was really worn down, she wondered if she was valuable to God. Her marriage was also on shaky ground at the time.

During these difficult times, her horse Gus had been a stabilizing force in Robin's life. At the end of the day she couldn't wait to wrap her arms around the gray gelding. It was almost as if he felt the turmoil she carried in her heart from the horrendous things the children had endured. After brushing and saddling him, the real world disappeared when she put her foot in the stirrup and swung up. She entered a beautiful world riding a horse that loved her over grassy hills, around tall trees, and along a gurgling creek.

Robin looked into the mirror, double-checking her makeup before she went to work. She took a deep breath and focused her heart on the words scribbled there. "You are a mighty God." She paused and let the words sink in. It was Tuesday. Although the river was still way outside its banks, the rain had stopped. Over the last 24 hours, the water had subsided enough that many roadblocks had been taken down. After work, her husband would drive her out to the ranch—if the roads were clear.

After work, the sun shone brightly as John and Robin drove slowly down the storm-damaged roads in their silver Ford pickup. The truck bounced through new and old potholes. Whole sections of pavement had cracked and fallen away.

Robin's heart pounded harder and harder with each passing mile. She knew it would be a miracle if all their horses were okay. *Is Gus okay? Oh, Gus, you have to be okay!* In the back of her mind the doubt snuck in again. *Does God love me enough to do a miracle for me?*

When the pavement ended and the dirt road began, the truck sank deep into the muck. The engine roared and the wheels spun, flinging mud along the sides of the truck. Slipping and sliding as if they were on ice, they wound down the road. Robin leaned forward as the little empty farmhouse and the rusty tin barn came into view. She surveyed the area around the barn. The water hadn't gotten this high. They turned into the driveway and drove past the house. The truck rumbled as they drove over the cattle guard and down to the barn. Her hopes soared as she glimpsed a couple of horses standing under the eaves of the barn. But as they drove closer, she saw a couple of buckskins, a sorrel, and a bay. Her mind screamed, *Gus, you have to be here too!*

Robin pushed the truck door open. The rushing creek roared below the barn. Racing inside, she glanced around. *Five horses. There should be six. Everyone is here except Gus!* A wave of nausea crashed over Robin. She ran down the hill screaming, "Oh God, help me find him! I know that he has to be here!" There were only two options. He might be across the creek…or he'd been washed downstream.

The water had risen most of the way up the bank but had receded some, leaving behind the skeletal remains of downed trees. The brush and grass lay flattened. Robin cupped her hands to her mouth and screamed as loud as she could, "Gus! *Guusss!*" She walked along the fence line, getting as close to the water as she dared. *God, You've got to show me where he is! He's got to be here!* She scanned the trees on the other side. They had been underwater. Debris lay in piles everywhere. *Could the water have trapped Gus against the fence and then swept him away?*

Crashing water was all she could hear. She looked at its swirls. *Nothing could survive that.* She looked up and screamed with all her might, "Gus! *Guusss!*" *God, if he's here, let him hear me. Help him see me.* Five minutes passed. She paced along a finger of land between the fence and the water. *Dear God, let him be alive!* Trees bobbed down the creek. She squinted across the creek. "*Guusss!*" Tears streamed down her face. *Lord, he can't be gone. Help him hear me.*

Suddenly Robin heard a faint crash. She saw a flash on the other side of the creek. Her gray gelding raced toward her, his eyes locked on her. His long, silver mane and tail flowed as he jumped over logs and debris. She stood gaping. *He's okay! He's coming toward me. He's running! He's not hurt!*

He raced faster and faster, as if he'd been looking for her for days, and she was finally here to help him. The water raced, forming an impassible chasm between them. Robin expected him to slow and then stop as he neared the raging water. He stampeded to the edge and paused. His body shook as his neigh rang out. He launched off his hind quarters and plunged into the turbulent water. Robin held her breath. *Oh, God, don't let him be washed downstream...or be impaled by a tree!*

Only Gus's gray nose, wide eyes, and jawbone showed above the deep, dirty-brown water. He swam with powerful strokes, but the river swept him downstream. Trees and limbs floated alongside him. Robin followed along the bank. She cupped her hands and screamed, "C'mon, Gus! Gus!" He bobbed in the current. Slowly he moved toward her. Tears streamed down her face. "*Guusss!*"

Suddenly the horse gathered his feet underneath him, popped out of the water, scrambled up the bank, and ran to her. Brown water dripped off him, and he shook. Breathing hard and exhausted, he low-ered his head toward her feet.

Robin wrapped her arms around his neck. Her mind whirled through the things that could have happened. He could have tried to swim the creek when it was higher and been washed downstream. He could have gotten hung up in the barbed-wire fence that lay in a ball on the bottom of the creek. He could have been jammed with a stick or a tree. But Gus came through the ordeal unharmed! Dirty water soaked her clothes. She buried her face in his neck. "God, thank You for my miracle," she prayed aloud.

By the time the flooding was over, it had set new records for peak flood depths in 15 locations. It claimed many lives, including more than 31 human lives and countless ranch animals, domestic animals, and wildlife. The estimated property damage was more than $750,000,000. It was a once-in-a-lifetime flood.

For Robin it was a once-in-a-lifetime experience. Not only did she receive her miracle of God protecting Gus, but through that harrowing time she saw how much God cared for her. The greatest miracle wasn't watching God rescue her horse. It was what God did in her heart. She'd been living in the flood of life with emotional skeletons popping up and floating past. In the end, when Gus ran to her, Robin had been running to Jesus—trusting Him with all her heart—full blast… no hesitation. When she jumped into the river of His love, believing, He embraced her. In His arms she made a life-changing discovery. That day He showed her that if she trusted Him, no matter what else was going on He would take care of her and bless her.

· Robin and Gus ·

Over the next few weeks, God also con-firmed for Robin that she was touching the lives of the children she worked with in a mighty way. She summed it up when she wrote on her mirror, "I am the miracle." Without a doubt, she was important and valuable to God.

Robin triumphed over one of the devil's sneakiest schemes. It's when life is at its most difficult moments that he hits us the hardest. Out of his bag of tricks he pulls out the lie that hurts the worst because it wounds our hearts so deeply. It's a question followed by an accusation the devil whispers in our ears: "Do you really think you're valuable to God? Nothing you do matters." Believing that lie destroys hope. The devil knows there are days when he can wear down even the strongest people. He gets pleasure out of inflicting pain. He hopes that we will let his lies penetrate our hearts and wound us.

Jesus said, "Come to me, all you who are weary and burdened, and I will give you rest" (Matthew 11:28). Jesus lived here on earth temporarily clothed in a human body. He knows what it's like to have the devil grating on us. He knows that it's a dangerous time when we're emotionally weak. When we find ourselves getting worn down, that's when it's the most important that we run to Jesus just like Gus galloped to Robin...and Robin ran to Jesus. Walking to Him just isn't fast enough.

Lord, help me rest in the fact that You love me and
I am one of Your miracles. Amen.

· Thoughts to Ponder ·

Have you noticed that when you're worn down emotionally that's the exact moment in time when the devil hits you with ideas that wound your heart? At those times, have you wondered if you were valuable to God? Have you ever thought of yourself as a miracle? How can you rest in the fact that you are special to God?

25

DAZZLE

Replacing Fear

The Rocky Mountain peaks that rimmed the Flathead Valley were already covered with snow, and a brisk November breeze whispered through the pines. Although it was sunny outside, the weather forecast said a winter storm would move in later that day. Pulling my protective earmuffs on, I grabbed the pneumatic nail gun and stepped up a couple of rungs on the ladder next to the new addition on the barn. I was nailing up the last of the sheets of siding, and I wanted to get it finished before the storm hit and winter set in. I glanced across the pasture at the horses and mules that were munching down hay.

I wonder what Dazzle is going to do when she hears the nail gun? My other horses were used to the sounds of rifles, pistols, and other loud noises. I'd only owned the black two-year-old Tennessee walker mare a couple of weeks, so I wasn't sure how she'd react to the sharp report from the nail gun that sounded like a gunshot. *Will she take off running?* My fences were good and tight. She was familiar with them, so I didn't think she'd try to blast through them. But she might do a few laps around the acreage before she calmed down.

The air compressor kicked on, making a loud, sputtering noise. I pushed my safety glasses up on my nose and looked at Dazzle. Her ears were riveted toward me, but she kept eating. *Well, that's good. The noise isn't bothering her.* I leaned my arm against the sheet of siding I had tacked into place. With my other hand I pushed the tip of the nail gun to the siding and squeezed the trigger. Pop! The nail shot true. I paused. My earmuffs silenced the world. Out of the corner of my eye I checked on Dazzle. The mare continued eating like nothing had happened. *Well, that's easy.* I shot a few more nails. Still nothing from Dazzle.

After a few minutes I abandoned my concern about the horse. Locked into my muffled world, I clung to the ladder and drove lines of nails down the siding. Suddenly a warm breath brushed my back and something bumped me. Shocked, I grabbed hold of the ladder and turned. Dazzle stood at the base of the ladder cocking her head side to side, looking at me and the siding. I burst out laughing. Instead of being afraid of a new and unusual experience like most horses are, Dazzle was curious. She bobbed her head at me as if asking what I was doing. Balancing the nail gun in the hand that held on to the ladder, I reached down and stroked her forehead with my free hand. "I'm nailing on the siding so you'll have a place to get out of the wind this winter."

She smelled the gun and then looked at me.

I laughed. "Okay, silly, although you really should be wearing protective eyeglasses. I'll show you what I'm doing." Pressing the tip of the gun against the siding I squeezed off the trigger. *Bang!*

My mare stretched her nose forward and smelled the siding where the nail had gone in.

I rubbed her nose. "See, isn't that awesome?"

I pondered her reaction as I climbed down the rungs and scratched her neck. I could take some lessons from her. When I face new, unusual, or uncertain things in life, I've sometimes reacted in fear and withdrawn. *How many opportunities have I missed out on because I did that?* I wondered. *Fear dissolves my hope for a better future. Why do I jump to fear as my first reaction instead of being curious like Dazzle?* That thought ran through my mind for the next couple of days. The truth became so clear when I read Romans 8:15: "The Spirit you received does not make you slaves, so that you live in fear again; rather, the Spirit you received brought about your adoption to sonship. And by him we cry, 'Abba, Father.'"

Throughout the Bible, God commands us to "fear not." We're to look at the world through eyes of faith, which fills us with hope. My focus in difficult situations was my choice, and I'd chosen fear. I can change my response any time I want to. I decided it was time to make a conscious decision to develop my curiosity so I will be fueled by hope.

> *Lord, show me areas in my life where I hold back*
> *because of fear. Fill me with so much curiosity*
> *that I brim with hope. Amen.*

· Thoughts to Ponder ·

When you're faced with uncertain circumstances, what is your first response—fear or curiosity? Why do you usually choose that? What would a reaction based on faith look like?

26

FORGING AHEAD

Breaking Free

The door on the 1972 Chevy pickup truck groaned in protest as Wendy slid onto the driver's seat and pulled it shut. She turned the key. The truck belched to life, blowing a cloud of exhaust into the cold air. The engine rattled as the tires crunched through the snow. Wendy shifted into first gear and pulled into the narrow lane. She was headed to the top pasture where her husband, Gary, who was standing in the back of the pickup, would toss out hay for the horses while she inched the truck forward. She glanced in the rearview mirror. A small group of young mares restlessly wandered in the corral. This day would be the first time she'd feed this little band in this pasture. She watched the new mare. *God, watch out for Dandy. Please lead her so she finds her way around her new surroundings.*

Back in the fall, Wendy had purchased Dandy as a broodmare. She'd searched high and low for some good bloodlines to add to her breeding program, and this mare's pedigree was tops. She would also add a rare and beautiful color to Wendy's herd. She was a "grulla," meaning she had tan-gray fur and a dark dorsal stripe that ran along the top of her back from her black mane to her tail. She even had black "zebra" stripes on her legs. The best part was that the owners had been selling the mare at a drastically reduced price. They said it was because of an injury she'd had on a hind leg, which left behind some bulging scar tissue. Wendy was familiar with that type of wound. It wouldn't interfere with the mare's ability to be a good broodmare, so Wendy purchased the horse sight unseen. But the owners hadn't divulged the mare's biggest handicap.

A light breeze had rustled the golden aspen leaves when Wendy unloaded Dandy from the shipper's trailer. She led the horse toward the barn. The mare quietly followed her. But when Wendy turned to go through the gate, the mare walked straight ahead and slammed into the wooden fence. Shocked, Wendy's heart sank. Carefully she guided the mare into the barn and performed some simple eye tests. The mare was blind.

Wendy was crushed. *Lord, where am I going to find the time to take care of a blind horse? How will she fit in?* Blind horses often have to be confined in a stall to avoid being injured by other horses. Wendy stared at the beautiful mare and knew in her heart that God had sent her horses so she could be their caretaker. Maybe Dandy was one of them.

Wendy scheduled an evaluation with the veterinarian. He didn't believe the horse's blindness was a genetic condition, and he gave Wendy a thumbs-up to use Dandy as a broodmare. Even though it was late in the year, Wendy bred the mare to her stud.

At first Wendy kept Dandy in a small run so she could acclimate to the surroundings. Wendy's goal was to have the mare become part of her herd, but in the back of her mind concerns nagged at her. *Would Dandy be safe with the others? Could she negotiate the pastures and fences safely? Would the other horses accept her?*

Wendy soon realized her new mare had been kept in a small pen all her life and had never been in a herd. The next step was to introduce Dandy to the small group of young mares confined in the corral outside the barn. Leading her through the gate and letting the mare go, Wendy was shocked when the horse stepped among the other horses with an air of confidence. Dandy's tan-gray ears tipped with black hair were constantly tuning into her surroundings. She seemed to ignore the concept of a pecking order among the herd. At feeding time she stepped up to the hay without hesitation, a brave thing for even a sighted horse to do. For a blind horse it was an act of faith. It was almost as if nobody had bothered to tell the mare she was blind.

Once Dandy was established in the band of mares, Wendy decided to turn the small herd loose in a bigger pasture for the winter. She opened the necessary gates, and then started up their old pickup. The

Chevy rattled as it chugged over the snow and up the lane toward the big pasture. Gary stood in the back of the pickup, his voice being jarred by the bumpiness as he called to the mares. "C'mon, girls! C'mon, girls!" Although he'd swung the gates open from the corral to the lane, the young mares were milling around the small enclosure.

Wendy frowned as she watched them. *Why aren't they coming?* The truck crawled into the pasture. Gary tossed flakes of hay on the ground and called some more. "C'mon, girls!" The horses watched and saw the hay, but they still held back.

Wendy angled the truck so she could observe the mares. *Why aren't they moving?* She glanced through the herd. Dandy stood close to the barn. Cautiously she shuffled through the snow until her nose touched the wooden rail that lined the top of the fence. Using her whiskers and nose, she slowly followed the rail toward the truck. Wendy watched in awe. The mare's ears were swiveling as they traced Gary's voice even as she held her face next to the wooden rail. Feeling her way slowly, Dandy walked into a corner and made the turn. She paused when she got to where the gate had been closed. She tipped her nose back and forth, exploring the empty space. It was new territory for her. Carefully she stepped down the lane and headed toward Gary's voice.

What happened next astounded Wendy. As Dandy passed the other mares, they slowly fell in line behind her. They had been milling around because they were waiting for their leader to go first! In spite of her severe handicaps, Dandy hadn't just fit in, she'd become the herd mare, the top horse the others looked to for leadership.

· Dandy and her foal ·

When Wendy told me the story about Dandy, I was spellbound. The mare had led with confidence even though she carried scars from the past—her ill-healed leg and her blindness. She hadn't let her inadequacies keep her from forging ahead. I sipped my tea. *What if people went through life like that? What if we refused to let the scars of the past and any perceived disabilities hold us back? What couldn't we accomplish!*

The Bible reveals more than one person who refused to let the past hold him or her in bondage. In the Old Testament, prostitutes were looked down on. That's why the one person who has always baffled me is Rahab, who was a prostitute (Joshua 2–6). Despite her unsavory occupation, she helped the Hebrew spies escape from the town of Jericho and put herself in danger. To my amazement, Rahab is mentioned in Matthew 1:2 as the mother of Boaz, who is in Jesus' genealogy! I shake my head in wonder each time I read that.

Rahab is a perfect example of how God's grace and mercy covers our sins and weaknesses—no matter what they are or how deep they go. There's hope for all of us. As soon as we cry out to Jesus and ask Him to be our Lord and Savior, He helps us discover our future in Him. If God doesn't hold us back because of our disabilities or our past, why should we?

*Lord, show me how to live each day with confidence,
forging ahead to accomplish the dreams
You've placed in my heart. Amen.*

• Thoughts to Ponder •

Have you felt inadequate because of your past—the mistakes, any disabilities, some inabilities? Have those feelings stopped you from pressing in and achieving your dreams? Have you considered that God is able to work through you, flaws and all? Have you asked Him to do that?

27

SHORT LEGS

What's in Your DNA?

The Minnesota sun stood high in the deep-blue sky, casting its bright rays over the rolling fields of the Saint Croix River Valley. It was a perfect day—Saturday and school was out for the summer. At the horse stables, inside a wood-railed arena, a dozen teen girls sat on their horses waiting for the lesson to start. Some milled around practicing last week's lesson, and others clumped in groups chitchatting. The girls had taken lessons together at this stable for several years.

At one end of the arena a few riders on horseback stood in a semi-circle. One of them, 13-year-old Jami, relaxed in her western saddle enjoying the warmth of the sun and the conversation. She gently stroked the neck of her chestnut-red horse named Honey. As the conversation lulled, a younger gal with sandy-blond hair and a tough disposition cocked her head and looked at Jami's horse. Her voice cut like a dagger through the conversation. "Boy, she has short front legs!" A high-pitched laugh slithered from her lips. The other riders stared at Honey. They nodded in agreement and whispered. Jami wanted to crawl into a hole. She bit her lip. *Is Honey built awkwardly?* The words burned into Jami's heart. She looked at the ground. It was true, but she'd never noticed it before. The other girls gawked at Honey like she was a freak.

Honey had been Jami's Christmas present several years ago. Standing only 13-hands tall, the horse was the perfect size to climb on and ride bareback. From her cross-breeding of a hackney pony and Morgan horse, she had a willing-to-please attitude. By the end of their first summer of lessons, Honey would do anything for Jami. Her trot was so smooth they almost always won the competitions where the rider balances an egg on a spoon while trotting across the arena.

Perhaps the words about Honey's short legs stung so badly because Jami loved her so much. Although Jami tried to ignore the words, they simmered in her mind. It wasn't until years later that she made an exciting discovery about Honey during the middle of winter.

Jami had always wanted to drive a horse and buggy. Maybe it was all the Westerns and the *Little House on the Prairie* episodes she'd watched as a kid. She bundled up and headed out to her dad's pole barn. Digging through dusty leather straps, she found the perfect ones to craft a homemade harness so Honey could pull her on the toboggan. The cold air nipped at Jami's cheeks. With mitten-covered hands she rigged up the makeshift harness. Honey stood quietly waiting and watching. Her breath rose like steam from her nostrils in the cold air. Jami put the harness on Honey, connected the toboggan, and then crunched through the snow as she led Honey down the driveway and out into a big, open field. Although the toboggan bumped behind Honey, she didn't seem to mind.

The sun sparkled over the endless fields of white. Jami brought Honey to a stop in the center of the pasture. Jami rigged the reins and then sat on the toboggan. The snow creaked as the sled sank into the snow. A twinkle sparkled in Jami's eyes. She gently slapped the reins and said, "C'mon, Honey!"

Honey stepped forward, but as soon as she felt the weight of the sled she stopped. She'd been trained to give to pressure, not to push into it.

Wiggling the reins, Jami called again, "C'mon, Honey!"

Honey stepped forward until she felt the weight of Jami on the sled. Confused, she reared up a little, as if saying, "I can't pull against this. I'm not supposed to pull against something restraining me." Dropping back to the ground, she curled her neck around. Her big, brown eyes questioned her friend.

Determined, Jami continued tapping. "C'mon, Honey. You can do this. Let's go! C'mon, Honey!" The horse nervously shifted her feet, but then she lunged forward. The toboggan jolted, throwing Jami's weight backward. Jami got resettled, and they were off! Around the field they went.

Honey is a natural, Jami thought. *Of course! The hackney breed is used as carriage horses.* They were bred with short but powerful front legs to be smooth-gaited while pulling. Honey's short legs were an asset—a quality breeders strived to achieve…a gift.

The sled cut through the snow. The cold wind sprayed snowflakes into Jami's face. She giggled and laughed as they bounced around the field. That is, until they turned down the driveway to go home. Honey trotted faster and faster, and the toboggan slid easily across the plowed snow. There was something Jami forgot to consider—how to stop the sled so it wouldn't run into Honey.

Jami tugged a rein to turn Honey to the side. The horse veered sideways. The teen pulled both reins to stop her and then bailed off the sled. Jami tumbled to a stop, and Honey kicked the sled to a stop. The stop definitely needed some perfecting, but the short-legged horse was perfect.

Has anyone spoken disparagingly about you or someone you love? Words can hurt, and often our interpretation of them causes us to feel shame and anger. Then the devastating emotions get buried in the deep recesses of our hearts, where they wreak havoc when similar situations arise.

The interesting part is that the very thing that is being made fun of is often the very thing that makes you unique and special. Although the girl made fun of Honey's short legs, that trait was tucked inside Honey's DNA by God. When Honey became a driving horse, she was doing what she'd been bred to do.

Have you wondered what God tucked inside your DNA? Ephesians 2:10 says, "We are God's handiwork, created in Christ Jesus to do good works, which God prepared in advance for us to do." God planned our gifts and talents *before* we were born. It's up to us to join with Him in a lifelong voyage of discovery to find those special niches He's carved out for us.

When Jami discovered Honey was a natural at pulling, she bought a real harness, and her father restored an antique doctor's buggy for her.

Honey loved driving so much that Jami barely had time to gather the reins and get on the seat before the horse trotted down the driveway. And Honey never slowed down until she returned home! Her head would swing left and right as she enjoyed the view and proudly did what she was created to do.

• Jami and Honey •

Lord, open my mind to how You've created me. Give me the courage to pursue what You want me to do. Amen.

• Thoughts to Ponder •

What has God put in your DNA? What gifts and talents has He given you that might be buried because of hurtful words or painful experiences? How can you start using your gifts and talents for the Lord?

28

DEE GIRL

Anxiety Attack!

A light breeze rustled the tall evergreens that lined both sides of the road leading to the farm in the Maine countryside. Down a small hill, an antiquated red barn stood on the left and small, grassy paddocks were on the right. Beside them, in a large green field, a dozen horses were grazing in the afternoon sunshine. Wearing her barn coat, Cheryl walked into the ancient-smelling barn, picked up a halter, and walked down the aisle between the wooden stalls. She'd boarded her horse here at Selena's place for several years, and she sometimes helped do chores.

A deep and robust nicker greeted Cheryl as she approached one of the stalls. She grinned and then heard the horses outside answer with whinnies. Although the black mare in the stall was nearly 30 years old, Dee Girl was still the herd mare.

After buckling the nylon halter on Dee Girl, Cheryl led her out of the barn toward one of the smaller paddocks. The mare's hooves clip-clopped on the dirt road. The horses in the big pasture raised their heads and watched them. Because Dee Girl was so ancient she was kept in a small paddock next to the big field. She was currently serving as a nanny for a young horse. Suddenly Dee Girl stopped. Cheryl glanced back. Something was horribly wrong.

The mare looked like she was having a seizure. Her body shook. Her eyes grew wide. Every muscle stiffened. Her breathing sped up but then became shallow and labored. Within seconds the shaking stopped and the mare stood as if she were frozen.

Cheryl gasped. *What happened? This is Selena's favorite horse. Nothing can happen to her!* She stroked the old mare's neck. Under the fur, the skin felt cold and clammy. The horses across the way milled around the fence, pacing as they watched Dee Girl. A wave of panic crashed over Cheryl. *What am I going to do? What's Selena going to do?* She had to get the horse to walk 30 feet to the paddock so she could turn her loose and run for help. Wiggling the lead rope, she urged the mare forward. Dee Girl's head hung low. In slow motion she lifted her head as she dragged one front foot forward. She appeared woozy. With concentrated effort she propped her leg a little to the side, swaying off balance as her muzzle nearly hit the ground.

Cheryl inhaled deeply. *What am I going to do if she falls over?* The mare's breathing was erratic. It seemed like an eternity before Cheryl managed to coax the mare into the paddock. Once inside, Dee Girl stood with her head hanging low, her legs propped at angles to hold her up, her breathing heavy and raspy. It looked like it took all her effort to not fall over.

Cheryl knew this was the end of Dee Girl's life. Thirty was old for a horse. A battery of worries assaulted her. *How is Selena going to take this? Do I stay with Dee Girl? Do I run and get Selena? What if Dee Girl falls over when she is here by herself?*

Dee Girl shifted her feet and planted them more solidly. After taking a deep breath, she raised her head and looked at Cheryl, as if releasing her to get help. Cheryl sprinted to Selena's home, a short ways from the barn.

Hearing the news, Selena immediately called the vet, who said she'd come right over.

After examining Dee Girl, it was determined she'd suffered a stroke and wouldn't recover. With tears streaming down her face, Selena made the decision to put Dee Girl down. The vet said she'd come back that afternoon, and Cheryl offered to return later to support Selena.

A wave of anxiety assaulted Cheryl as she drove home. *What happens when a horse is put down? Will I be able to be strong for Selena? What's the herd going to do without Dee Girl? Who would they look to now? How are Selena's kids going to take this? And what am I going to tell my daughter?* Doubts assaulted her as rapidly as machine-gun fire.

Several hours later Cheryl drove down the long road lined by evergreens. She parked by the barn. A huge pile of dirt was heaped by the backhoe. Dressed in coveralls, the veterinarian and Selena stood in the paddock. Tears streamed down Selena's face as she stroked her favorite horse. The old black mare's head hung low.

Gravel crunched under her feet as Cheryl walked to the paddock. Dee Girl didn't even raise her head. The horse was only a shadow of what she'd been only hours earlier. Wanting to give Selena the last few moments alone with her horse, Cheryl stepped into the barn. Under the cover of the weathered wood, she cried and prayed. *Dear Lord, I don't know what to do.* When she paused, anxiety dealt a cruel blow to her heart. Pain was like spears being thrust into her. She closed her eyes and proclaimed aloud, "Please, Lord, give me strength." Almost instantly she heard in her spirit, "Walk out of the barn." She recoiled. She wanted to stay in the barn until it was over. But the thought nudged her again.

Cheryl stepped into the afternoon sunlight. Selena and the vet slowly led Dee Girl out of the paddock. Step-by-step the horse struggled to drag one foot in front of the other. With each step Dee Girl grew closer to the paddock containing the herd. Then Cheryl watched a miracle unfold. In the paddock the most dominant horse stepped next to the fence and hung its head over the rail. Then the next most dominant, all the way down the pecking order until every horse stood lined up shoulder-to-shoulder. It was as if God had taken His hand and gently brought each horse up to the fence, one at a time. There wasn't any biting, nipping, or squealing. Instead they all stood at attention, honoring Dee Girl. The peace of the Holy Spirit washed over Cheryl.

With each step Dee Girl drew closer to the line of horses she'd dedicated her life to protecting. She lifted her head higher and higher until she looked like the black beauty she'd once been. Her mane gently tumbled over her neck. Gracefully she arched her tail. When she was even with the first horse, she stopped, turned her head, and whinnied. It was as if Dee Girl passed the torch by appointing a new herd mare, saying, "You're going to have to step up." That horse—and only that horse—proudly answered. Dee Girl took another step and focused on the next horse. Her voice sounded different as she whinnied this time. The second horse answered. Down the line of horses Dee Girl went, calling with differing tones to each one, and each horse answered. Was Dee Girl giving them final pieces of advice? All stood in line, their shoulders nearly touching until Dee Girl walked past, and then they slowly faded into the pasture.

Those moments are etched in Cheryl's memory as a miraculous answer to prayer. She'd let anxiety strip her of her courage and take her on an emotional roller-coaster ride. But when she gave her fear to God, He set her free and gave her His peace. It was as if God was showing her that the only thing she had control over was herself. Everything else He had in His hands.

In the past I've struggled with anxiety. When situations looked bleak, I turned to worry, as if worrying could change anything. If ever there was a time for a person to worry, it would have been when the disciples watched Jesus get arrested and sentenced to be crucified. Only the week before, Jesus' fame had soared. The crowds had honored Him by waving palm branches, singing, and dancing when He rode into town on a donkey (John 12:12-15). They had waited thousands of years for the Messiah to come to save them. Jesus, the Messiah, was finally positioned to take His place as king of the Jews. And now this? In a couple of days He would be crucified?

What were the disciples thinking as they watched their Savior die on the cross and their world crumble around them? It was the perfect setup for an anxiety attack. Did they wonder, *How can this be? What will happen to us? Will the world tumble backward into darkness? How are we going to explain this to the other believers? Did we believe in the wrong man?*

From the world's standpoint it looked as if all were lost, as if Jesus the Messiah wasn't real. The world looked so dark that perhaps the disciples worried God wouldn't want to save it. Their hopes were crushed. But everything was happening according to God's plan. During those bleak moments, Jesus knew what His disciples would be facing. That's why on many occasions He'd warned them that He would die and God would raise Him from the dead. The words of wisdom He gave to Peter in the Garden of Gethsemane still apply today: "Watch and pray so that you will not fall into temptation. The spirit is willing, but the flesh is weak" (Matthew 26:41).

When Cheryl followed Jesus' advice by praying and giving her situation to God, He set her free from anxiety, filled her with His peace, and refueled her hope. The good news is that He'll do the same for you today.

Lord, when I'm tempted to worry, remind me to run to You for wisdom and comfort. Amen.

• Thoughts to Ponder •

Is there something you're worrying about today? Do you have a long list of things that torment you? Our God is the God of comfort and answers. He'll lead you to the perfect solution if you'll pray, listen to His still small voice, and follow His advice. Why not pray right now?

29

SWEAT EQUITY

Diligence

The announcer's voice blared through the sound system and carried through the massive indoor arena. The folks on the sidelines cheered for the competitor. Sand sprayed into the air from the horse's hooves as it raced through a cloverleaf pattern around the three barrels. In a small paddock beside the main arena, a cluster of contestants and their horses waited their turn to ride. Kristi sat deep in the saddle. Her chestnut-and-white paint mare shifted her feet, antsy to get going. For Kristi, one of her main goals hinged on this run. If she and her horse, Dreamy, got a top score, she'd qualify to compete at the National Barrel Horse Association World Championship Race, usually referred to simply as "The World." This was an honor awarded to only a few. The World is one of the toughest barrel racing competitions. Only the best and most athletic horse and rider teams are chosen according to their cumulative scores of the races they'd run that year.

Kristi's thoughts swirled as she looked at the beautiful horses surrounding her. Many were expensive ones that carried famous bloodlines and were trained by top professionals in the industry. They were way out of her league. She and Dreamy were the underdogs. If they qualified, it wouldn't be because of expensive bloodlines or high-dollar trainers. It would be because of years of hard work, tears, and prayers. Kristi wiped her sweaty palms on her blue jeans and prayed. *Lord, wrap Your angels around us. Keep us safe from danger or any injury. Let us have a fast and fun run. Amen.* Kristi leaned forward in the saddle and stroked Dreamy's neck. She gathered the reins and whispered, "All right, girl. You've got to make your mama proud."

Years ago, Kristi had gotten Lacey, Dreamy's mom. At that time Kristi was a horse-crazy teenager who worked in her family's floor covering store after school. Every spare moment was spent at the barn, living and breathing paint horses so she could barrel race. Her best friend and soon-to-be-husband, Dwight, wanted to buy her a second horse, so he took her to a catalog horse sale. When she got out of the truck, she spotted a chestnut-and-white paint being lunged in a pen. Instantly she knew that was the horse she wanted. The mare had been bred with cow horse and speed bloodlines. When it pranced, it exuded an air of power, confidence, and majesty. Kristi could see herself winning while riding her. She was thrilled when she was the high bidder and the auctioneer's voice rang out, "Sold!"

Then the nightmare began.

When Kristi walked Lacey to her horse trailer, the mare seemed skittish and head shy. And she limped. After picking up the sore foot, Kristi discovered that the horse was wearing an egg-bar horseshoe, sealing off the frog part of the hoof from contacting the ground. She'd never seen anything like them before. A warning bell rang in her mind. *Is there something really wrong with her feet? If there is, I can get out of the sale right now.*

She led the mare to the back of the trailer.

The paint refused to load. She threw up her head and braced her feet.

Kristi tried everything she knew of, but nothing worked.

A tall man wearing a starched, white dress shirt, starched jeans, cowboy boots, and a hat offered to help. He said he was the horse's former owner. The whites of the mare's eyes showed as soon as he took hold of the lead rope. Suddenly he wielded a whip. He beat the mare's legs and face. The mare reared and fought to get away.

Kristi screamed, "Stop it! Stop beating her!"

Finally he quit.

After he left, Kristi calmed Lacey and eventually coaxed the horse into the trailer. Any thoughts of canceling the sale had been dispelled. She knew she needed to do the right thing for the mare too. She wouldn't send the horse back to a man that beat her for anything.

After consulting her veterinarian, Kristi discovered that Lacey had been drugged before the sale and most likely would be permanently lame. In spite of the mare's abuse, the two became best friends almost immediately. Kristi resigned herself to the fact that she would be the caretaker of the horse for the rest of her life. Even though the mare couldn't do anything productive for her, Kristi doted on her friend, giving her supplements to help with her hoof problem. She even trailered the horse miles away to a specialty farrier. On one of those visits she shared with him that she'd been trying to raise a colt out of her other mare, but year after year the mare didn't get pregnant.

He grinned. "You ought to breed Lacey to my stallion. It would make a great barrel racing prospect."

Kristi went to see his stallion and was awestruck. She hadn't considered breeding Lacey, but why not?

During the pregnancy, Kristi loved to slip into Lacey's stall at night. In the cool evening air she'd wrap her hands around the mare's belly and, in a singsong voice, Kristi would chatter to the baby in the womb. "I can't wait to meet you." The mare would turn her head sideways and bat her long eyelashes. Her days of abuse in the past were erased.

Kristi had studied and memorized every stage of a horse's pregnancy and delivery. The week before Lacey was due, Kristi and Dwight, now her husband, shoved together six bales of hay to make a bed for themselves in the aisle outside Lacey's stall. They wanted to make sure they were present when their first foal was born. The February air was so cold they could see their breaths as they bundled up in their sleeping bags. Night after night they shivered as they tossed and turned. Every time the mare moaned, Kristi flicked on the flashlight and peered over the half-stall door. Then one morning at 2:30, Lacey lay down and her water broke.

Kristi could barely contain herself as she watched the amniotic sac poke out. She yelled, "Dwight, it's happening."

Dwight jumped out of bed and flipped on the lights. The other horses in the barn groaned as they woke up.

Kristi and Dwight huddled by the stall door and watched in

fascination. Kristi brimmed with excitement. "Is everything happening exactly like it's supposed to?"

Dwight held his finger to his lips. "Yes. Be quiet."

"Are you sure?"

Over the next few minutes Lacey lay in the wood shavings. The muscles in her belly contracted, and she groaned. The foal's front legs and nose, draped in the gray amniotic sac, protruded. Suddenly the horse rolled on her belly and jerked to her feet. The filly sucked back inside the mare.

Kristi's eye's widened. *Don't stand up! You need to be lying down!* she thought.

The mare circled in the stall, as if she were repositioning herself. Then she lay down. With a couple more pushes, the wet filly was born. Steam rose from her body. The amniotic sac hung around her neck like a robe. She lay on her tummy surveying her new world.

Kristi grabbed two towels and immediately took inventory as she wiped down the baby. Like her mother, the filly was a chestnut-and-white paint. She had a white streak that looked like a lightning bolt that started at her front shoulder and extended down her leg. Perhaps it was an outward expression of the speed bundled up inside of "Painted Dreams Come True"—"Dreamy" for short.

The emcee's voice brought Kristi back to the present. He announced, "Next up, Kristi on Painted Dreams Come True."

• Dreamy and Kristi •

The mare shook with excitement as Kristi reined her into the arena. Slowly Kristi guided the horse in a circle to get her attention. Then she leaned forward and kicked her. The mare knew what to do. She shot forward like a rocket. Kristi gave the mare her head. Sand sprayed from the horse's hooves. Running flat out, the mare carved around the first barrel and raced for the second. She shaved around the second and third barrels, and then beat a straight path to the finish line. It was a good, clean run!

Kristi screamed with excitement when the announcer's voice read off her score and placement. She had qualified to compete in The World!

Only God could take a permanently damaged mare and pair her with a gal who wouldn't give up to make miracles happen. I marvel when I think of the years Kristi sacrificed to take care of Lacey, a physically damaged mare. When life looked tough and it was obvious it wasn't going the way Kristi had planned, she didn't take the easy way out and dump the mare. She saved Lacey from a man who abused her.

Kristi never gave up hope. Instead, she tackled life day by day and steadily did what God led her to do through His Word and through her spirit. Her response reminds me of an insightful Scripture: "Do not despise these small beginnings, for the LORD rejoices to see the work begin" (Zechariah 4:10 NLT). To me it seems like God witnessed her diligence and years of sweat equity, so He paved the way for her to reap an unexpected reward—her dream horse—so she'd be able to compete at the National Barrel Horse Association World Championship Race.

Lord, when things aren't going the way I planned,
please show me how to be diligent and handle
situations Your way. Amen.

• Thoughts to Ponder •

What do you do when one of your plans goes awry? Do you toss it out the window? Do you think God might use that situation to bless you like He used Kristi's situation to bless her? Have you prayed and asked Him to show you what to do?

30

DOUBLE TROUBLE

Hope and Love

It was deathly still in the kitchen. Andrea set down her fork and help-lessly glanced at her three daughters who sat at the table. Her heart ached as she noted the dark circles under 11-year-old Bethany's eyes. *What happened to the giggling little girl that I love?* Andrea wondered. Bethany's eyes seemed sunken, and they looked dull from lack of nutri-tion. Her facial features appeared drawn and sharp. Only a few months ago she'd looked exactly like her healthy and happy 65-pound twin sis-ter. Now she was down to 45 pounds. Bethany had morphed from a loving child into a zombie who had lost more than 30 percent of her body weight.

Bethany sat at the table in a fog.

Under her breath Andrea prayed. *Lord, what can I do for Bethany?* She was grasping for a thin thread of hope. After a minute of contem-plation, Andrea became exasperated. She leaned forward and com-manded, "Bethany, you are going to eat this food. You're not moving away from this table until your lunch is eaten!"

Bethany's shoulders shook as she sobbed. Her blond hair hung in her face as she stared at her plate.

Out of sheer frustration, Bethany's twin sister, who was sitting next to her, scooped up a fistful of food and tried to cram it into her sister's mouth.

Bethany gagged and spit out the food. Although she sat at the table until the meal was over, she never ate a bite.

Even though she reprimanded Bethany's sister, Andrea wanted to scream in agony. She'd constantly prayed for help and guidance, but she couldn't figure out what to do. Her daughter was dying in front of her eyes.

This bad situation had started in the fall after the twins turned 11 years old. Andrea was struggling with a mysterious illness thought to be cancer and homeschooling the girls. Andrea and her husband, Richard, noticed that Bethany seemed detached from the family.

Before the doctors figured out what was happening, Bethany's weight had plummeted to 45 pounds. Only a shell remained of the once-bubbly child. The unspeakable had struck their family. Anorexia seemed to have a death grip on Bethany.

Frantically Andrea tried to grasp the reality. *Bethany is only 11 years old! God, we've done everything we can to raise her in a godly manner. How can this happen to our family?* In desperation she prayed, *What can we do? Please guide us to help for Bethany.*

They enrolled her in an anorexia clinic. Andrea was thrilled that the staff understood the disease and had a plan to help. They sent Andrea home with meal plans and suggested that she find an activity Bethany could get involved in—something where she could excel and find hope. At that point, Andrea expected that in a short amount of time Bethany would gain weight and life would return to normal. But that's not what happened.

Bethany would have nothing to do with the plan. She'd become so depressed and withdrawn that she didn't care if she lived or died. Every time Andrea suggested an activity, Bethany merely shrugged. She grew weaker every day. Her heart beat was fading away. At the last visit to the clinic, the staff had told Andrea that Bethany would need to start eating or they would have to hospitalize her and insert a feeding tube to keep her alive. Those words haunted Andrea. She lived in constant prayer.

One January day while Andrea was in her bedroom folding clothes, Bethany came in to get a book. They chatted a few minutes, and then Andrea asked what she could do to help.

Bethany replied, "I hate feeling like this. I used to be happy. I want to feel like that again."

Andrea reminded her that faith in God had always been the most important thing in her life. She asked if Bethany would like to pray with her.

Reaching for each other's hands, they bowed their heads and prayed for three miracles: that God would take away Bethany's hurts; that He would restore her joy for living; and that He would give her a desire to eat.

A few weeks later Andrea made spaghetti and meatballs for dinner at her parents' home, which was next door. The family sat on bar stools around the large island in the kitchen. Everyone but Bethany was eating.

Andrea's mom's brown eyes twinkled. "I saw a flyer at the post office. They opened a horse ranch down the road, and they're offering horse lessons. I thought you girls might like it."

Andrea watched a thin line of a smile wiggle across Bethany's face. Hope sparked inside Andrea. She was scared to death of horses so the twins had never ridden, but if it would help Bethany, she'd make it happen. She figured the girls would take a few lessons and move on to something else. But God had a bigger, totally unexpected plan for their family.

Andrea, her sister, and the twins drove over to the ranch on a damp and cold Missouri afternoon in March. When Andrea watched her fragile daughter step next to a sorrel horse with four white socks, she whispered a prayer. *Oh, Lord, make this work.*

Bethany learned how to clean the horse's hooves and how to groom the animal. Then the instructor had her climb on bareback.

Breathlessly Andrea watched as the trainer lunged the horse at a trot. Her heart sank as she watched Bethany bob up and down on the sorrel's back barely able to stay on. *That looks miserable*, she thought. But when Bethany slid to the ground, Andrea noticed she wore a smile on her face from ear to ear.

The morning of the next lesson, Bethany awoke excited. The shadow of a girl began connecting with the world again.

Weeks later one of the doctors at the clinic noticed Bethany had improved a little bit. He asked what was different.

Andrea replied, "The only thing I know that's making a difference is that she's riding horses twice a week."

The doctor nodded. "Let's focus on that. Let's see if it will help make her better."

Andrea's heart soared. She left the clinic with strict instructions for Bethany's program. She would not be allowed to ride horses unless she followed the meal plan.

Although Bethany started eating bites of food, her recovery was painfully slow. She remained in critical condition from starving herself so long. Her body had to readjust to digesting simple foods.

By the first of April, the twins had ridden a horse at the barn that was for sale. Andrea had watched the color of life blush her daughter's sickly white cheeks. She believed this horse thing might be their last hope to pull Bethany through. The previous months of anorexia treatment had drained Andrea and Richard's financial resources, so Andrea prayed about buying the horse. They scraped together enough money to buy it, thinking the twins would share.

Within the first few days it became evident that the horse and Brittany were a team. Bethany was left on the sidelines.

Weeks later the horse trainer at the stables casually mentioned, "My mom's got this horse for sale. It's a nice one. You might want to go look at it."

Andrea thought, *Richard's not going to like this. How can we afford another horse? We already have one horse we never planned on owning.*

On the drive home, Bethany looked at her mom with sad eyes. "Mom, can we please go look at her?"

A week later, Andrea pulled the gold Ford Explorer into the driveway of a stately ranch house surrounded by pastures lined with white rail fences. A red-dun quarter horse stood tied under a tree by the barn, slick and shiny. Andrea glanced in the rearview mirror at Bethany. The girl almost glowed when she saw the mare.

Before they headed home that day, the horse had affectionately rested its head on Bethany's shoulder. At that moment a miracle had taken place. A bond of love had been forged between Bethany and the mare.

Andrea knew this was the horse God had planned for her daughter Bethany, but the price was three times more than what she'd expected.

On the ride home, Bethany asked, "Mom, do you think we can buy her?"

"We really don't have that much money to spend on a horse." Andrea gripped the steering wheel. "Your dad and I are going to have to talk about it. We'll have to see what we can do."

After much discussion Andrea and Richard came up with a plan. Their immediate resources were tapped dry, but they decided to sell their investments. They did, and two weeks later they bought the mare. And they've never regretted it.

Honey gave Bethany something to hope for and to love. Bethany gained weight, and the spark of life glowed in her eyes again. Through the power of God and the love of family and a special horse, Bethany recovered. God's hope and love broke the chains that anorexia had on her life and set her free. Psalm 33:18 breathed life into this family: "The eyes of the LORD are on those who fear him, on those whose hope is in his unfailing love, to deliver them from death and keep them alive in famine."

When Andrea prayed to God, being willing to do whatever He wanted, God revealed to her an unusual answer—horses. Andrea never would have dreamed up this solution on her own, but she was open to the leading of the Holy Spirit. As she followed Him, a seed of hope was birthed in her heart. That same hope wiggled its way into Bethany's heart. It blossomed and bore the fruit of love when Andrea and Richard followed God's leading and were willing to risk selling their investments to help their daughter.

The love God placed between Bethany and Honey carried the teenager further than anyone imagined. His plans are so much bigger than ours! He doesn't want us to just survive; He wants us to thrive. On Memorial Day 2009, the ranch held a big celebration. The twins breathlessly watched a trick rider do gymnastics on her horse to music. Like all teens who are impressed with something, it wasn't long before Bethany and Brittany were working with a trainer and learning how to safely stand on their saddles while their horses trotted around the arena.

Encouraged by their trainer, they soon added trick riding lessons from another trainer to their schedules.

The two girls thrived on the challenge of learning to ride a horse full-speed while performing gymnastics. They practiced six hours a day. Within a year, the twins were performing as "The Double Trouble Trick Riders." Recently their younger sister, "Lil Yodelin Libby," has joined them. They've gone on to thrill audiences throughout the United States with their daredevil horseback riding. Since starting horseback riding in 2009, they've been featured in many venues, including the United Rodeo Association, the American Royal Youth Rodeo in Kemper Arena, the Cody Wyoming Nite Rodeo, and the American Finals Rodeo Association.

• Bethany and Honey •

God took a family that was beaten down and battling the devil's stronghold of anorexia and transformed each member through the power of His hope and love. Now the family has a mission—to encourage others so they will also know that with God there's always hope.

*Lord, when I feel trapped in hopelessness, please remind me
that You are the way, the truth, and the life. Amen.*

• Thoughts to Ponder •

When you face a hopeless situation, do you ask God to lead you out of it first thing? How can you keep your eyes open for opportunities He might be presenting to you when you're struggling? How will you handle difficulties better next time?

31

STICKY FEET

Consistency

The rays of the March sunshine warmed my back as I ran my hand down Wind Dancer's hind leg. My sorrel mule cocked her leg, shifting the weight to the other side. I tried to pick up her foot, but she wouldn't release it. I lightly tapped her leg. "C'mon, Wind Dancer, pick up your foot." She stood like a bronze statue. I groaned. *Not again! Didn't we just cover this ground last week?* She has what's known among mule owners as "sticky feet." She acts like all four feet are cemented in place when she doesn't want to cooperate.

I'd been working with Wind Dancer 35 minutes a day, every day, for the last two weeks. The farrier would be coming out to trim her hooves in a couple of weeks, and last time he had a wrestling match with her. I felt horrible for him and was totally embarrassed by my mule's lack of manners. So each afternoon I'd bundled up in my tan Carhartt bib-overalls and jacket after spending a long day at work and went out to stand beside my mule. I'd like to say "work with my mule," but really I didn't have much to show for it. Wind Dancer still refused to give me her feet. Only last week God had encouraged me to feed her a round slice of carrot as a reward when Wind Dancer cooperated. She'd responded well for a few days, but now her feet were stuck again. Only this time one leg was half-cocked. *God, what's her problem now? How long is this going to take? Will she ever pick up her feet for me?*

Patiently I held my hand on her left hind leg. "Yoo-hoo! Wind Dancer, I'm still here. Did you forget about me?" Gently I squeezed the chestnut on her lower leg and then released the pressure. The leg lifted ever so slightly, but then she quickly put her weight back on it.

Excitedly I stood up and chimed. "Good girl! I knew you could do it!" Quickly I fished a carrot slice out of my pocket. Scratching her neck, I reached my left arm under her jowls and over her nose to draw her face toward me to give her the carrot. But she tossed her head and backed away. Astonished, I stared at her. In my spirit I heard, "She doesn't trust you as her leader. That's why she won't give you her head or let you pick up her feet."

My red mule stood braced with wide eyes as she looked at me. I stood there in shock. I'd never even considered that Wind Dancer didn't trust me. *Why, I'm the one who raised her...and planned her from conception. I talked to her the whole time she was in her mother's womb. I'm the only person she's really known her whole life. How can she not trust me?*

I stepped next to Wind Dancer and scratched her neck. In my spirit I heard the answer: "You haven't been consistent with your training. Consistency is what develops trust in the leader." I sighed. I knew I hadn't been working with my mule regularly. I'd done that when she was a baby, but since then I'd taken on an intense, full-time job in town. I'd devoted myself to learning the new job thoroughly while my horses and mules stood around in the pasture. Once I was out of the routine of working with them, I'd merely spent time with them during feeding time.

Wind Dancer was a well-behaved *friend*, but I hadn't done anything to develop a teacher–pupil relationship. The good news was I'd invested the last two weeks building it. The bad news was that I had a long way to go.

I looked into her soft-brown eyes. "Okay, girl, we're going to work on you trusting me to move your head." Once again I stood with my left shoulder next to her right shoulder. I reached my left arm under her jowls and scratched her cheek. I gently moved my hand over the top of her nose and paused. Slowly, with very little pressure, I guided her head toward me. With my right hand I poked a slice of carrot into the corner of her mouth.

My mule's glance darted sideways, looking at me. I could almost hear her say, "What are you doing?" She pressed her lips tightly together.

I pushed the carrot further in with my index finger. The slice disappeared.

When she tasted the carrot, her eyes lit up. They said, "Wow! Is that all you wanted? All I have to do is let you move my head and I get a carrot? Do it again!"

After half a dozen times, as soon as I guided her head to the side, Wind Dancer would pucker her lips and wiggle them as she groped for a carrot slice.

Chuckling, I poked one more slice into her mouth. "Next we're working on your hind feet," I announced. I stepped to her rear and rested my hand on the top of her hip. She shifted her weight to the other side. I lifted my eyebrows. *Nice. This might not be difficult at all.* I ran my hand down her leg. Before I got to her hoof, she picked up her foot and let me hold it. *Wow! Once I got her to trust me with her head, she trusted me with her feet. Hmmm.*

When I was finished working with her, I handed Wind Dancer the last carrot. She chewed it up, flipped back her top lip so her teeth showed, and nodded toward me. I'm sure she was saying, "Thanks, Mom! Those were great!"

· Wind Dancer saying, "Thank you!" ·

Over the next couple of weeks I continued to work with Wind Dancer daily. When the farrier set his tool bin next to her and reached for her hind foot, she placed it in his hand. He was shocked, and my heart soared! I hadn't wasted all that time! The consistent effort applied to my hope that she could learn had paid off. As her leader, I'd built up her trust in humans.

Thoughts about her sticky feet drifted through my mind the next couple of days. *My consistency in training Wind Dancer is so much like my relationship with God.* It reminded me of 1 Corinthians 9:25-26: "Everyone who competes in the games goes into strict training. They do it to get a crown that will not last, but we do it to get a crown that will last forever." The apostle Paul understood the power of training. As I reviewed the past few years of my life, I noticed that when I put effort into making time for Bible study and prayer, I'd grow. I started out as a person who had sticky feet when God asked me to do something. I'd known God for years, but I would lock my feet and stand like a statue because He'd been a great friend but I didn't trust Him as my leader. As I became more consistent in my Bible study, I got to the point where I was ready to step out in faith the instant I realized what He wanted me to do. But it wasn't until I meditated on Him and learned more about Him from His Word that I could confidently say, "Yes, Lord" when He asked something of me. When I let Him turn my head toward Him, I started trusting Him in a deeper way. Consistency is a powerful asset.

Lord, show me how to be consistent in following You. Amen.

· Thoughts to Ponder ·

What do you think the correlation is between being consistent and developing trust?

When God asks you to do something, do you have sticky feet? Or perhaps you stand with one leg cocked *almost* ready to cooperate? What would help you develop more trust in your Lord?

32

AGAINST ALL ODDS

Attitude

Snow crunched under Wendy's and Gary's boots. Vapor rose from their mouths and noses as they breathed in and out. Wendy cracked open the heavy, wooden door and they entered the tall, 100-year-old, timber-framed barn. Although they'd installed a big heater in there, the air was still crisp. From the back stall they heard a high-pitched nicker from one of their two-week-old colts. He was the happiest colt Wendy had ever had. She had dubbed him Big Red shortly after he was born. When he was just a week old, his red body was the size of a typical month-old colt.

Another happy nicker drifted through the barn. Gary and Wendy looked at each other with a question in their eyes. *Maybe today is the day we can make a positive decision.*

With a hesitant heart she walked to the back stall and peeked in. The red colt grunted and chortled as if nothing was wrong. Wendy pursed her lips and braced her heart against the possible reality. *Lord, what do we do? Should we put him down?*

Mariah stood over her colt. Big Red lay on the golden straw. He raised his head, but his body remained prone. His bright-brown eyes followed any movement Wendy made. It had been six long days since the colt lay on the floor and couldn't voluntarily move any part of his body below his neck. The weather had dipped below zero, and to keep the unmoving colt warm, Wendy had wrapped him in a "Redneck Blanket." She'd pulled a hooded sweatshirt over his front-end, threading his limp front legs through the arms. On his rear-end she'd used a thermal top, putting his hind legs through the arms and his tail through the neck hole. Then she'd tied the two together. Even that hadn't been enough. Hour after hour Wendy had knelt on the floor next to him, massaging his cold legs so the blood would continue to circulate through them.

Big Red was born a healthy, happy, frolicking colt. Then a week ago, while doing her rounds to check on the mares and colts, Wendy had discovered him lying in the pen unable to move. It was almost like he'd been paralyzed, but instead of his body being stiff, it was like Jell-O. Wendy had raised horses for more than 30 years, and her mind clicked through the list of possible illnesses and diseases. She'd examined him and found he had a fever so she'd started him on antibiotics and prayed that he'd recover. Every hour and a half around the clock she and Gary had gone out to the barn to lift him under the mare so he could nurse. They were exhausted from only getting in catnaps and discouraged because even though his fever was gone, the colt remained helpless.

Steam rose from Big Red's nostrils. He chortled as if saying, "Oh good! You're here. I'm so glad. Hurry and pick me up. I'm hungry." The colt was growing so fast that he was almost too heavy for the two of them to lift. Gary squatted next to his front end and wrapped his arms underneath. Wendy wiggled her arms under the colt's back end. On the count of three they heaved him waist high.

The colt's body hung like a wet dishrag, but that didn't seem to dampen his spirit. Big Red acted as if life was great.

Wendy and Gary lugged the colt next to Mariah's side, his small hooves dragging through the straw. The mare curled her head back and nickered to the colt. He excitedly whickered in return.

Wendy briefly closed her eyes. *How can you both be so happy?* she wondered. When a colt is sickly or dying, the mare often abandons her offspring. But Mariah was hanging in there, whispering encouragement to her baby and watching over him like he was the most precious gift she'd been given.

Gary balanced the deadweight of the front end as he looped his arm over the withers and under the belly. The mare moved her hind leg to the side so Gary could lift and guide Big Red's head toward the mare's teats.

Before the colt was latched on, he circled his lips and sucked. His curly whiskers wiggled. When he firmly connected, he voraciously gulped, never spilling a drop.

After he was filled up, Wendy and Gary lay him back on the straw and changed his little outfit. Wendy knelt next to him rubbing his legs, wondering how long they'd have the energy to keep doing this.

Throughout that day and night nothing changed.

The next morning at breakfast tears welled up in Wendy's eyes. She looked at Gary and said, "If Big Red's not better today, we've got to put him down." He agreed. When they were done eating, Wendy's heart felt sick. She slipped out the door with the words, "I'll see you in the barn."

The temperature had dropped so much that her boots squeaked through the snow. She threw her weight against the heavy door to push it open. It rumbled on its track. Big Red's whinny echoed through the old barn. Her shoulders slumped as she walked outside his stall and peeked in. He lay on the floor excitedly talking to her. The straw around his head looked as if it had been raked aside. She knew why. Only a couple of days ago she'd cried as she watched the colt try to move. With his big body wrapped in the sweatshirt and thermal top, he'd flopped his head like a fish out of water as he tried to propel himself across the floor. But only the straw moved. Big Red had tried so hard, but his muscles refused to work.

She opened the stall door. Waiting for Gary, she sat on a bale of hay looking in. *Lord, I need Your wisdom. He can't go on like this. He hasn't moved his body in a week. What do You want us to do?* Through her tears she watched Big Red nod his head and continue his happy greeting.

The colt batted his long, black eyelashes. Suddenly, in one movement he curled his legs underneath him, rolled onto his belly, and jerked to his feet. The clothes hung from his body. Big Red stepped toward his mom tripping on the sleeves.

In astonishment Wendy jumped to her feet. *He's standing!* She ran into the stall sobbing. "Oh God, thank You!" She quickly peeled the clothes off Big Red. With awe she watched him walk to his mom's side, brushing against her. He bent his neck, reached under her, and suckled as if he'd been doing it every day. The mare curled her head around and nuzzled his rump. Wendy wiped the tears from her cheeks. "Thank You, God!"

Wendy had watched a miracle. The only explanation was that the power of God healed the colt. Today when she talks about Big Red she says, "He was such an example of how to handle the worst-case scenario. We don't know—even in that last minute—how things can turn around." She shared with me that Big Red's attitude controlled the whole situation. If he would have given up at any point in time, she would have

· Big Red and his mom, Mariah ·

put him down. But his positive attitude had encouraged them to keep hoping. She believes his attitude inspired his mom to stick with him too. Through the ordeal, God gave Wendy a priceless message: When there's not a glimmer of hope in sight, God and your attitude will determine the outcome.

When I think of people whose attitude contributed to the outcome, the star that shines in my mind is Joseph. Wow! In the book of Genesis there are 13 entire chapters about this one man! Obviously God wants us to know about Joseph's life.

When he was a teenager, Joseph was betrayed by his jealous stepbrothers and sold into slavery. But he didn't wail and moan about being a victim of circumstances. Instead he focused on God, which gave him hope. The people his brothers sold him to then sold Joseph to an Egyptian named Potiphar. "The LORD was with Joseph so that he prospered" (Genesis 39:2). Potiphar was very pleased with Joseph and trusted him with his household and everything he owned.

Potiphar's wife, however, wanted to have an affair with Joseph. When he refused, she falsely accused him, and her husband had Joseph cast into prison.

Even then Joseph didn't lose heart and quit. "The LORD was with him…and granted him favor in the eyes of the prison warden. So the warden put Joseph in charge of all those held in the prison" (39:21-22).

Joseph stayed faithful to God, and God stayed with him, eventually orchestrating Joseph's release from prison, his rise to becoming second in charge of Egypt, and the one who saved his family, including his treacherous brothers, from famine.

I marvel at Joseph's amazing faith and attitude. By concentrating on God and working diligently, he went from a slave and prisoner to being a top official in Egypt.

Through Big Red's attitude of hope and Wendy and Gary's faith and diligence, the red colt grew into a strong and healthy horse. He was never sick another day and experienced no residual effects of his illness. When it came time for Wendy to send in his registration papers, she proudly penned his official name: Against All Odds.

Lord, when the odds are stacked against me, remind me that my faith in You and my attitude help determine my future. Strengthen me with courage to face every adversity with faith in You, hope, and a positive heart. Amen.

• Thoughts to Ponder •

Have you been betrayed by a friend? How did you respond? If you could go back in time, how would you change your response? How do you maintain a positive attitude and press forward in your day-to-day life?

33

THE MISFIT

Being Unique

Large ceiling fans blew the hot and humid air through the sanctuary of the small country church. Voices echoed off the arched wooden ceiling as people visited among themselves before the service started. With her elbow resting over the top of a pew, Bonnie was turned sideways to talk to Laurie who sat behind her. Enthusiastically Bonnie waved her arm. "Can't you just see it?" she exclaimed.

Laurie leaned forward and nodded.

Bonnie and her husband had retired and moved to this small community that was located in the lake country of northern Minnesota. Bonnie, a talented pianist, had already drawn the small church together through music. She'd formed a choir, and on the Sunday of the Fourth of July they'd put on a musical production. The church and the community had been thrilled.

Now Bonnie was organizing a "live nativity" program for Christmas. A lot of folks hadn't heard of such a thing, but her excitement was contagious. She talked about how the long U-shaped driveway in front of the church would be perfect. The cars could enter one end of the "U" and exit the other, stopping at the individual stations where the folks in the church would be acting out Christmas scenes. Bonnie nearly glowed as she paused, dreamily envisioning the evening's celebration.

Instantly, Laurie envisioned Joseph and Mary on the way to Bethlehem. Joseph would be leading a donkey with Mary sitting on its back. Swept along in Bonnie's enthusiasm, Laurie said, "Well, we've got a donkey."

Bonnie smiled. "Great!"

All of a sudden Laurie realized what she'd said. It was true she had a donkey. But the critter had been eating grass in the back pasture for years since the grandchildren had outgrown her. *Was she still tame enough to ride? Would she even let someone lead her around? Worse yet, what if she pulled some of her donkey shenanigans?* Although the donkey was a lovable teddy bear, she had been a challenge since she'd been given to Laurie and her husband.

Laurie remembered that day all too well. A blue-sky, spring day, Laurie's husband had been working outside. When he came in he mentioned casually, "By the way, a guy jogging by said, 'I see that you've got horses. Do you want a donkey?'"

Laurie asked, "And what did you say?"

"I didn't say anything. I thought you should know though. The man told me who to contact if we decide we're interested."

Laurie hadn't ever owned a donkey, but she thought the idea sounded fun. Reasoning that her baby granddaughter could ride it, she called and discovered that it had been a pet at a local kids' camp. A couple of days later she and her husband drove over to see the donkey. They pulled up to a corral that contained one lone animal—a short, brownish-gray donkey with enormous white spots. It laid its floppy ears back, lifted its nose, and brayed, "Hee-haw. Hee-haw." Its whole body shook and its ears flopped with the long, drawn-out honking noise. Laurie giggled. The fuzzy critter looked like a big teddy bear! The donkey stood a little over waist high. Laurie glanced at the donkey's feet and grimaced. They looked like they'd never been trimmed. The hooves had grown so long that they curled up like skis. Laurie petted its shaggy coat. The poor gal looked like such a pitiful misfit. She needed to take it home. The first thing she would do was change its name. Laurie shook her head. *Who would name a donkey Martha Stewart?* So she dubbed it Annabelle or simply Donkey.

Laurie figured out right away that donkeys aren't horses wearing a different skin. From the core of their beings they are polar opposites. Instead of moving away from pressure, Annabelle would push into it. Anytime Laurie asked the donkey to do something she didn't want to, the donkey would stiffen all four legs slightly splayed out and refuse to budge. Then she'd throw her head in a big circle as if shaking her head and saying, "No!" Even the seemingly simple task of leading Annabelle resulted in a major production. The donkey refused to move unless they strung a rope behind her rear-end. And dealing with her hooves? Almost impossible! No wonder they were curled like skis. The farrier Laurie hired charged her an extra five dollars—per kick.

Finally Laurie started to understand donkey thoughts. The little fuzzy beast was afraid of everything unfamiliar. Once Donkey understood that she wasn't going to get hurt, she was okay. Soon the animal's personality blossomed. When Laurie was cleaning the barn, Donkey would sometimes sneak up from behind and put her head under Laurie's armpit begging for attention. Donkey loved stealing Laurie's husband's hat out of his back pocket. Over the years the donkey proved to be a great ride for the grandchildren. But she still was a misfit.

· Annabelle ·

Laurie's stomach churned as the date of the live nativity drew closer. She shared with Bonnie her concerns about Annabelle's donkey vices. Bonnie merely grinned and said, "I'll be praying for Donkey."

And indeed she did. A few weeks later at one of the preparation meetings that Laurie wasn't able to attend, Bonnie rallied the whole group to pray for Donkey. She led the prayer with "Lord, you know Annabelle. You made her."

From that moment on, Donkey became kind of a mascot to the church. Folks kept asking Laurie, "How's Annabelle?" And a crazy thing happened. All of a sudden Annabelle became a gentle and sweet donkey. She didn't have any of her usual donkey vices. On the first night of the production, Donkey even loaded easily into the horse trailer!

Mid December when Laurie and her husband drove up to the church on the afternoon of the first production, it appeared that Donkey was cooperating but the weather wasn't. A winter storm burst forth with freezing rain and snow. The lawn of the church bustled with activity even as folks bent against the wind and rubbed their hands to keep warm. They put the finishing touches on the lights that were strung from the trees. As dusk settled, everyone took their places under the glowing lanterns. At the first stop, the pastor and his wife stood bundled up against the pelting rain. They would greet each carload of people with an explanation of the tour and offer a gift bag that contained a New Testament and a coloring book.

Then cars would pull forward to an open-sided, wooden hut. Under a spotlight, "Luke" sat at his desk writing the Christmas story on scrolls. Next was Laurie as Mary, dressed in a big skirt and seated on Annabelle, who was being led by Laurie's husband dressed as "Joseph." Following them, some shepherds stood around a campfire. Nobody in the community had sheep, so they used goats instead.

An innkeeper sat at the No-Room Inn. Next was a spotlight that shone brightly in the top of a tree to illuminate a local tree-service guy dressed up as an "angel of the Lord." He would periodically blow a trumpet that would blast through the cold night air announcing Jesus' birth. Then he'd wave at the people.

A spectacular stable scene came next, featuring another Mary and Joseph, the baby Jesus, and a few miniature donkeys. The last stop was a choir singing Christmas carols. Their beautiful melodies drifted throughout the whole production.

Laurie took a deep breath as one of the guys made a stirrup with his hands. She stepped up and straddled Annabelle. Slowly the headlights of the cars pierced the darkness and pulled into the U-shaped driveway. For the next two nights, through sleet and snow, Annabelle calmly carried Mary back and forth to "Bethlehem." Annabelle would stop when a new car would drive up. The people were excited to see Mary on a real, live donkey. They asked questions and snapped pictures. Annabelle didn't even mind the flashes from the camera!

Over 100 cars wound around the U-shaped driveway during the two evenings. Not bad for a community of only a couple hundred people. People's lives were touched, and a misfit, floppy-eared donkey finally found her place in life—a starring role in the Christmas story.

When Bonnie emailed me the picture of Annabelle carrying Mary, I instantly fell in love with the little spotted gal with gargantuan ears and a loud hee-haw. Misfits play big parts in God's plans. Look at the variety of people God included in His Word. Most of the disciples weren't handsome or famous. Many of them were sweaty fishermen—working-class people. Ordinary men God worked through to accomplish extraordinary things. God carries that same theme through to completion, revealing that His thoughts are opposite of the world's. Most kings of the world rode magnificent horses, but God chose a lowly donkey to carry His Son to Jerusalem. On His celebrated ride, Jesus rode the misfit of the equine kingdom (Matthew 21:2-5). The apostle Paul marveled about the lowly misfits God chooses to work with and through:

> My dear friends, remember what you were when God chose you. The people of this world didn't think that many of you were wise. Only a few of you were in places of power, and not many of you came from important families. But God chose the foolish things of this world to put the wise to shame. He chose the weak things of this world to put the powerful to shame (1 Corinthians 1:26-27 CEV).

Those misfits whom God has chosen resemble uniquely shaped pieces in a jigsaw puzzle. The picture won't be complete without all of us. Like Annabelle in the Christmas play and sweaty fishermen who became disciples, each of us has an important role to play in carrying the good news of Jesus Christ to the world. No matter how lowly or how much of a misfit you think you are, there's a place for you in God's plan!

Lord, reveal my role in Your great plan. Amen.

• Thoughts to Ponder •

Do you feel like a misfit? That you're on the outside looking in? Have you considered that your unique qualities make you an asset in God's kingdom? How do you think God wants you to use your special traits and abilities for Him?

34

GENTLE HEARTS

Gentle Giant

The clop, clop, clop, clop of Honey's hooves on the dirt shoulder of the road drifted through the small, rural neighborhood in Minnesota. Fields of green grain carpeted the rolling hills. Seventeen-year-old Jami took up some slack in the reins as her chestnut-red horse drifted toward the upcoming driveway. Jami chuckled. Ever since she'd started selling Avon from horseback, Honey had turned into a social butterfly. She insisted on turning down every driveway because she knew there might be a kind lady who would offer her an apple or a carrot.

Jami glanced down the driveway and spotted Janet, a good friend and close neighbor. She was playing with her nine-month-old son, Drew, on an expanse of freshly mowed lawn in the center of a circular drive. Jami guided her mare down the driveway. She stopped Honey at the edge of the lawn. The saddle creaked as she dismounted. After dropping the reins, she dug an Avon catalog out of the saddlebags. Honey knew the routine. She instantly lowered her head and cropped the lush, green grass.

Jami smiled at Drew as she strolled toward them. The baby was sitting on the lawn in a T-shirt, diaper, and bare feet. He grinned at her and giggled.

The warm summer sun lulled Jami and Janet as they browsed through the catalog and chatted about their past week. Jami glanced over to check on her horse. She stared in amazement. Honey was still nibbling on the grass, but her large, brown eyes were locked on Drew. The baby sat inches away from Honey's nose. Jami's mind ran wild. *Oh my gosh! He's right there! That's dangerous!* She knew any sudden movement might scare Honey, and she could accidentally trample the child. She held her breath as the next few moments seemed to unfold in slow motion.

The chunky, blond-haired and blue-eyed infant was enthralled with his new discovery. Instead of slapping the horse with waving hands like most infants do, Drew was carefully exploring her face with his pudgy fingers. Honey slowed her chewing. It was almost as if the mare and child were silently communicating with each other. Gently the child traced her nostrils and stroked the white furry star on her forehead. Placing a hand on either side of Honey's nose, he clung to her bridle.

• Jami's horse Honey •

Jami froze. *How will Honey take someone yanking on her bridle?*

Hand over hand the child pulled himself up halfway and teetered.

Jami's heart raced. *Oh my! He's climbing up her face! Honey won't like that. I've got to do something—but what without scaring her or startling Drew?*

Drew pulled himself all the way upright.

Jami, relieved at Honey's calm manner, looked over at Janet.

Janet wasn't upset at all. Instead she seemed entranced by the beauty of the moment.

An almost palpable bond was being woven between the child and the big, red horse. Wobbling, Drew grabbed Honey's ears, one in each hand, to steady himself. He wiggled his bare feet. He rocked forward and back. Honey didn't flinch or move a hoof. She seemed to be enjoying his curiosity. After what seemed like eternally long moments to Jami, Drew plopped on the grass and found something else to explore.

Jami breathed a sigh of relief, but the wonder of those moments still captivates her. *How can a creature so big and powerful as Honey be so gentle?*

That's the same question I often wonder about God. How can a Being who created galaxies and hung the stars in place be so gentle and kind with me...with us? The explanation is *agape* love. In the Greek language the New Testament was written in, *agape* refers to God's kind of love—complete, unconditional, and unwavering. It's hard to understand the depth of that kind of love without looking at Jesus. He reflected the nature of God while He walked on earth (Hebrews 1:3).

When I'm reading the New Testament, one of my favorite stories is found in Matthew 19:13. The people were bringing their children to Jesus so He could bless them. The disciples tried to shoo the parents and children away, thinking Jesus was too busy to waste time on children. But Jesus told them, "Let the little children come to me, and do not hinder them, for the kingdom of heaven belongs to such as these" (Matthew 19:14). Jesus never pushed children away; He always welcomed them with open arms.

These words become extra special when combined with John 1:12: "To all who did receive him, to those who believed in his name, he gave the right to become children of God." Wow! Once we've accepted Christ as our Lord and Savior, God looks at us as His children. His gentle heart overflows with love for us. Like Drew with Honey, we can get up close and personal with God and explore who He is without fear.

There are many times when I read through the Bible that I'll come to a passage that befuddles me. I'll pause to consider the teaching. I often feel a kinship with Drew when he explored Honey's face. I cling to a few words, like Drew did to Honey's ears, and roll them over and over in my mind as I ask God to reveal His wisdom. Then the warmth of joy radiates through my spirit as God welcomes my innocence and curiosity. He always impresses the answer on my spirit. Like Honey towering over Drew, God towers over us, but He is gentle and never pushes us away. The most powerful Being in the universe has the gentlest heart of all. He wants to be our best friend and guide.

Lord, please reveal Your gentle heart. Amen.

· Thoughts to Ponder ·

Do you think of God as being all-powerful yet gentle very often? Do you agree that He welcomes your curiosity about Him? Have you looked at yourself as a child going to your heavenly Father when you have questions? What would you like to ask Him? Why not ask Him now?

35

SNICKERS

The Circle of Love

The back door slammed shut. Heather, who was sitting at the kitchen table, glanced up at nine-year-old David. Tears were streaming down his thin face as he rushed inside. His back was hunched over from scoliosis. His tousled black hair fell into his eyes. He paused and stammered, "I'm a throwaway kid." Sobbing, he rushed into his bedroom.

When Heather heard another door shut, she guessed David had hidden in the closet. His mournful wails pierced Heather's heart and tears welled up in her eyes. *Lord, how can I help this hurting little boy?*

Heather and her husband, Josh, had been foster parents for 10 years. When their last daughter graduated high school, they decided to quit fostering. By a fluke encounter, a local foster care and adoption agency found out about their experience and begged them to consider doing it again. After replying to the many phone calls with firm no's, they prayed about it again. They felt led to become recertified.

Shortly after that, the agency called about a little boy who needed an interim home while they searched for a permanent place. Heather replied, "I'll talk it over with my husband."

The man at the agency, Matt, said, "This little boy is nine years old. His name is David."

Heather rested her head on her hand. *Oh, you shouldn't have said his name*, she thought. *Now he's not just an anonymous kid; he has a name.*

Matt explained that for a year the boy had been in a home that planned on adopting him, but the father had hit the child. "Would you take him for a couple of weeks?"

Heather shocked herself when she said yes. That evening she greeted

Josh with the story and the news that Matt would be bringing the boy over the next day. Josh felt peace in his heart about the decision too.

It was a balmy Saturday morning in February when a gray car pulled into Josh and Heather's driveway. The sun glinted off the snow-capped Rocky Mountain peaks that towered over their pasture. They were in the corrals brushing the horses.

Matt unwound his six-foot, five-inch frame from the car. Weighing in around 265 pounds, he resembled a gentle giant. David scrambled out of the car and instantly hid his scrawny, 42-pound body behind one of Matt's legs.

Heather and Josh walked over, and while they greeted each other, Heather watched the wild-eyed child peek his head around Matt's leg. The boy's wide eyes showed he was terrified.

They all moved into the kitchen. As the adults chatted around the kitchen table, the boy sat and clutched his backpack. He was so thin that his brown eyes appeared sunken and were rimmed with dark circles. His elbows looked like knobs that protruded from his arms.

When Matt stood up to leave, David grabbed onto his legs. Matt gently pried the child's arms loose and set him in the chair. Bending over, he looked into David's eyes and said, "You have to stay."

David shook his head and wailed, "No!" He kept clinging to Matt, and Matt patiently continued to set the boy in the chair.

After Matt went out the door, got into his car, and drove away, David hugged his backpack and announced, "I'm not staying. I'm going home pretty soon."

When the boy went to bed the first few nights, he refused to climb under the covers. He wasn't going to settle in. He was barely willing to open his backpack, which contained some clothes and a cherished Green Bay Packers fleece blanket. During the daytime, David would fly into fits of rage over what seemed to be nothing.

The only things he showed an interest in were the horses. Every three to four hours when Heather would go out to check on their pregnant mare, she'd bundle up David. He'd go along but stood off to the side and watched. He wasn't going to get attached.

David kept telling Josh and Heather that he was going to be adopted by the other family and that he was going home soon.

Two weeks later the agency did take him back to his previous foster home. When they arrived, all his possessions had been packed in cardboard boxes and put out on the front porch. After loading the boxes in the car, Matt returned David to Josh and Heather's home.

That's when David had announced he was a throwaway kid and ran sobbing to his room. That was the day the nine-year-old boy knew he was homeless once again.

The painful cries cut through Heather's spirit. She rushed into David's bedroom and opened his closet door. The child lay on the floor curled in the fetal position. Tears streamed down Heather's face as she scooped up his bony body and clutched him to her chest. "Honey, you are home."

David struggled and screamed, "I'm not home! I'm a throwaway kid. Nobody wants me!"

Heather held him tightly. "You've come home. You're not going anywhere."

When Josh got home from work, Heather was still sitting on the bed rocking the crying boy in her arms. After sharing what had happened, Josh wrapped his arms around David and Heather. From that moment on, Josh and Heather knew David would be part of their family forever. They had no idea how God would mend the little boy's broken heart, but they knew He was the only One who could.

The next month the child raged, and it took hours to console him. Josh and Heather noticed that when they'd take David to the barn, he'd gravitate toward the pregnant mare. One day while feeding the other horses, they saw him walk over to the bay.

As soon as he got close, the mare dropped her head and nuzzled his tummy with her lips. Tentatively David touched her head and ears. The mare stood quietly. The little boy traced the white star on her forehead. His hands drifted down her cheeks. He drew her face next to his and kissed her soft muzzle. Wrapping his arms around her head, he hugged her. From that point on he loved on the mare daily. Usually the mare would wiggle her lips in pleasure.

A couple of weeks before the colt was due, Josh placed David's hand on the mare's tummy. When the colt kicked David felt it. Wide-eyed, he exclaimed, "What is that?"

Josh grinned. "A baby."

From that moment on, David couldn't wait for the foal to be born.

On a rainy April night, Heather donned her green Carhartt jacket and grabbed a flashlight to head out the door to check on the mare. Because it was a school night, she wanted David to sleep. Her boots slurped through the mud as she strode into the pole corral and flashed the beam over the horses. She shone it on the mare. One of the colt's hooves was already protruding! The baby was on its way.

Heather ran back into the house and woke up Josh and David. The three of them sloshed through the rain to the pole corral. They moved the mare into the foaling stall and flipped on the lights.

The horse walked in a circle and then lay down in the straw. Sweat broke out around her ears. She grunted and pushed. One of the colt's feet poked out again. David crawled next to the mare and scooped her head into his lap. As the mare groaned and shifted in pain, the alarmed David asked, "Does it hurt? Is it going to hurt her?"

Heather nodded. "Yes, she's hurting. But she'll be okay. This is how babies are born."

David cradled the mare's head, stroked her face, and patted her cheeks.

The mare heaved, and a little nose and foot showed. It looked like the other foot was stuck, which prevented the colt from coming all the way out. Between contractions, Josh reached in and grabbed the second foot. The baby swooshed out, and blood and amniotic fluid flooded the floor. The pungent smell of afterbirth hung in the air.

David's face contorted. "Gross! Oh gross!"

The gray amniotic sac lay like a sheet over the baby. David stared at the gray blob. He scrunched up his nose. "Oh that's icky." Suddenly he saw the colt inside flip an ear. The boy's eyes grew round. He jumped up and pointed. "Look! Look! Look!"

The colt shook its head and the amniotic sac settled around its shoulders.

David screamed, "It's a baby!" A smile spread across his face as he touched the colt's dainty ears and gently stroked its face. He hugged the colt getting the bloody, stinky slime all over himself, but he didn't seem to mind.

The mare lurched to her feet and nickered to the wet colt. The baby whickered in return.

While the mare licked the brown colt with a black mane and tail, Heather showed David how to rub him dry with towels. Enthralled, he watched the baby learn to use its stilt-like legs and slurp milk. A few drops dripped down the baby's curly whiskers and dribbled to the ground.

Before they headed back to bed, Heather asked, "Well, David, what do you want to call this baby?"

David's eye sparkled. He was thrilled that he was given the important job of choosing the name. Very seriously he raised his chin. "He looks like a Snickers candy bar. I want to call him Snickers."

Over the next month David nurtured the colt. Josh and Heather would look out the window and see Snickers and David romping through the pasture like a couple of puppies. If David disappeared, Heather usually found him out in the pasture sleeping soundly in the grass next to a napping Snickers. Heather knew God had used the colt to perform a miracle and mend the child's heart. David's emotions were healing. By giving his love to the mare and then to Snickers, David's heart was softened. Slowly he cracked it open and let Josh and Heather in.

· Snickers today ·

Years ago when I met David, I never would have guessed that the outgoing teenager had once been a hurting and withdrawn little boy. When Josh and Heather shared his story with me, I was stunned. Only God and His amazing love could have set up this situation. He chose Josh and Heather because He knew they'd be willing to love a child that so many had rejected. God orchestrated the circumstances so the agency would contact Heather and Josh. The Lord inspired them to get recertified as foster parents. And He had a hand in the mare getting pregnant and giving birth at the perfect moment in time so David's heart would soften and he could give and receive love.

The greatest example of the circle of love is demonstrated in the greatest love story of all—when God sent His Son, Jesus, to die for our sins and restore our ability to have an intimate relationship with Him. Jesus said, "'Love the Lord your God with all your heart and with all your soul and with all your mind.' This is the first and greatest commandment. And the second is like it: 'Love your neighbor as yourself'" (Matthew 22:37-39). When we take our eyes off ourselves and love God, and then we share His love with others, we complete the circle of love. That's when our hearts heal and God creates beautiful things, including forever families.

> *Lord, show me how I can help complete*
> *the circle of love in my situation. Amen.*

• Thoughts to Ponder •

Has your heart been shattered? Have you been hurt so deeply that you don't know if you'll ever recover? Ask God to reveal His love for you. When you understand how much He cares for you, ask Him for opportunities to share His love with others.

36

THE OL' PLUG
NAMED TORNADO

Patience

Late 1940s, outside Valley St. Claire, Saskatchewan, Canada

The prairie glistened, carpeted by millions of glittering snowflakes. The metal runners on the one-horse sleigh cut through the snow with a hissing sound. Steam flowed from the gray horse's nostrils as he drew the sleigh. The workhorse had been named Tornado by someone with a sense of humor. He was far from being a tornado. Although he was only 15 years old, he acted like an ol' plug. His nature, though, was more like an angel disguised as a horse.

The wind swept up snowflakes and dusted them over the passel of young children who sat in the back of the sleigh giggling and goofing off. The flakes stuck to their eyelashes and the scarves wrapped over their noses. Wearing a French-Canadian cap, their father sat on the front seat bundled up in warm clothes and wrapped in a blanket. He drove his children to the old country schoolhouse on the days when the weather was nasty, which was most of the time.

Louise was one of those children, most of whom were only a year apart. With four sisters and seven brothers, she fondly remembers their jaunts to school. Early in the morning her folks would heat up rocks on the old, wood cookstove in the kitchen. Her dad would harness Tornado and hook up the sleigh, while her mom would bundle up the children in mittens, scarves, and hats that she'd knitted. Many nights after the children were tucked into bed, Louise remembers falling asleep to the clattering of her mother's knitting needles by the flickering light of the kerosene lamp.

By the time Louise's mom pulled a "toque" over the smallest child's head, she'd be shooing her clutch out the door and waving them into the waiting sleigh. The ol' gray gelding would turn his head and peek from behind his blinders while the children were packed in the back. Hot rocks were placed at their feet and blankets were wrapped around their shoulders.

What happens when you stuff eight or nine little kids in the back of a sleigh? Surely they don't sit still! As soon as Tornado's hooves squeaked through the snow and the sleigh drew forward, the children bantered among themselves. The blankets fell from their shoulders as they laughed and nudged each other. Pretty soon they would be rough-housing. Moments later, one of the little stinkers would get mad and shove another one out of the sleigh. A scream would pierce the air.

Immediately ol' faithful would stop. He didn't even wait for the father to pull back on the reins. Tornado had learned that a scream meant one of his passengers was lying in the snow. He'd stop and slowly turn his head. Like a man looking over his reading glasses, he'd peek around his blinders. His wise, brown eyes would watch the child scramble to his or her feet and vault back into the sleigh. The horse wouldn't take a step forward until the child was settled in. Then the old guy would lean forward and the sleigh runners would once again hiss as they cut through the snow.

· Tornado, Louise, and a friend ·

Last fall Louise's eyes twinkled as she sat across the dinner table from me and shared stories about Tornado. None of the children ever got hurt when they fell out of the sleigh, and she didn't know how the horse put up with their shenanigans.

I chuckled and immediately a silly image formed in my mind. I pictured God rounding His children up in His sleigh. When we stay in the sleigh it's like when we're doing His will. But when we focus on other things, we fall out of the sleigh. Being human, we tend to make life more complex by bantering with God and each other until someone falls out or is even pushed out.

A great example of this is found in the book of Exodus. Moses saw an Egyptian beating a Hebrew slave so he decided to intervene. He ended up killing the Egyptian. Knowing it was wrong, he hid the body in the sand and hoped no one would notice. The plan backfired because some people had seen the murder. Moses escaped to another country to save his life (Exodus 2).

Instead of Moses asking God what His plans were and then getting involved with that, the Hebrew took matters into his own hands. He fell out of the sleigh. Later he climbed back into the sleigh, and God used him mightily to deliver the Israelites from Egyptian slavery.

When I reflect on my life, I see times when I've done something that caused me to fall out of the sleigh, I'm comforted by one of the greatest attributes of God—His patience! He patiently watches, and when I'm ready, He immediately stops the sleigh and invites me to climb back in. All I have to do is acknowledge why or where I fell, let Him know I'm sorry, and accept His forgiveness. Then I can settle back in for the heavenly sleigh ride.

God isn't looking for perfection. The only perfect person who walked planet Earth was Jesus. God is looking for willing hearts—people who will admit when they're wrong and then change their ways. People willing to ask for forgiveness and then jump back into the sleigh to give it another go.

God is love. And "love is patient, love is kind" (1 Corinthians 13:4).

Help me understand, Lord, the depth of Your patience and Your love so that I will always have the courage to turn to You and climb back into Your sleigh. Amen.

• Thoughts to Ponder •

Have you fallen out of the sleigh? Have you gotten back in yet? If not, what do you need to do to climb back in? How can you stay in the sleigh?

37

UNITY

Heart-Centered Relationships

Pat adjusted the headset for his microphone. Sweat trickled down his neck, and he took a deep breath. The sun was high overhead, and the Missouri air was sticky and humid. He stood in the round pen next to Evangelist and Prophet, his two black-and-white paint horses. The pen was set up next to a large circus canopy on the lawn of a country church. People milled around the grounds enjoying the Children's Fair.

Kids raced across green grass, chasing each other and screaming. Pat smiled as he watched the crowd move toward him. Some adults carried lawn chairs, while others gathered by the corral rails. As they settled in, he clicked on his microphone. "I'd like to thank everyone for coming out, and I want to thank the Lord for such a beautiful day."

The crowd quieted down, and all eyes were on Pat and his horses.

"I use horses to teach biblical principles. Today we're going to discuss the principle of unity and teamwork and how it applies to our personal lives as well as to the church." He knew the little community was suffering difficulties and many people were at odds with each other. That's one reason why he was here. Would his message make a positive impact?

Pat had lived the first few years of his life on a dairy ranch. Animals fascinated him. Although his family eventually moved to town, he never lost his love for animals. As a child he would curl up and read books about circus trainers and their training methods. Later he worked alongside horse trainers and became the assistant manager of a large breeding facility.

He became restless and dove into the rodeo world. He rode bulls and broncs—bareback and saddle. Then he made a decision to follow Christ. Although he attended church, he felt more like he was playing at it. He struggled with the concept of giving Christ free rein or lordship over his life. He'd received head knowledge about Christ, but his heart hadn't changed. He didn't have a *personal relationship* with Him.

Trying to fill the void, he set out to help others. He became a rodeo clown. He kept the cowboys safe after their rides on bulls and broncs. He inspired laughter in the crowds. The years rolled past, and the emptiness in his life became a deep crevasse filled with the skeletons of broken relationships and unhealthy behavior patterns.

His life changed when he was training horses at a Christian camp. There he was learning how to capture a horse's heart…and God captured his. While Pat was sitting on top of a mountain, God revealed His desire for a close relationship. Pat gave his heart to God, and God began to transform him from a broken-down cowboy into a cowboy with a vision to use horses to teach people about uniting their hearts with God.

A light breeze rustled Pat's striped shirt. The Lord had impressed on him that he was to do something he'd never done in the show before— something Pat deemed impossible. He was sure God was telling him to not put harnesses on the horses. He was to work with them without restraints. The mere thought of it stretched his faith. When horses are worked as a team, they have straps that tie them together to keep them synchronized. Pat also used lead ropes, lines, and reins to cue and guide them. On top of all that, Pat had purchased these two horses last fall so he'd only worked with them for a few months. The horses barely knew each other. Pat prayed and went forward, confident God knew what He was doing.

The two black-and-white horses stood in the round pen with bareback pads buckled on and halters without lead ropes strapped on. No other equipment was in sight. Standing in the middle of the round pen with a long horse "cue stick," Pat explained that he was doing something he'd never attempted. He was asking the horses to do their routine without hands-on guidance from him. He signaled to both horses to move left and circle the arena next to the rails. Both horses moved out in a trot, Evangelist in the lead with Prophet following behind.

The microphone crackled as Pat announced, "Horses are a great example of unity. But they have to stay together and they have to work together to glorify the trainer. God's our trainer." Pat used body language to ask one horse to slow down and the other one to speed up until they were side by side. They continued to trot in unison. Pat cued them to lope. "They have to stay focused on the trainer to keep him in the right perspective too." The crowd eagerly watched the horses as they cantered in step with each other. Pat motioned for them to stop. Gracefully they slowed and stopped. The audience murmured with approval. Pat breathed a sigh of relief.

After setting up a jump for the next routine, Pat's heart pounded. He looked down at his cowboy boots as he prayed under his breath. He was going to ask the horses to lope around the ring and jump the timber in unison. *Will the horses stay together without anything tying them together?* They would have to *want* to stay together and have the *desire* to obey him so he could direct them. He'd never asked them to do this. *Will they stay focused on me?* As he prayed, he felt the peace of the Holy Spirit wash over him.

Pat focused on Evangelist and Prophet. Stepping toward the horses, he cued them to trot along the rails. In a few steps they joined up with each other. Side by side the horses stepped up to a lope. Their black-and-white striped manes and tails waved behind them emphasizing their unity while they kept their attention focused on Pat and each other.

Everyone was silent while watching the horses and listening to the rumble of their hooves striking the ground. As the horses neared the jump, they adjusted their stride but kept their bodies rocking forward and back in rhythm. The crowd leaned forward with anticipation. Pat held his breath. Flowing together in almost one motion, the horses brought their hind feet underneath them and launched over the timber in perfect unison.

Ripples of oohs and ahs came from the crowd. A wave of awe

descended on Pat. His eyes watered a bit as he announced, "That's a perfect example of what true unity looks like."

As Pat was wrapping up the show, he felt led to do something extremely dangerous. He was sure God wanted him to stand on the backs of the horses with a foot on each one. Usually when he did this "Roman Riding," the horses were tied together and Pat held their reins. Without the straps, Pat had no physical control over the horses. If they spooked or decided to do their own thing, he would be in trouble. He could easily lose his balance and fall beneath them and get trampled.

Pat used riding showmanship to show how people and animals can work together. Over the years, he'd watched a lot of trainers use force to control their horses. He'd witnessed similar situations in human relationships. The horses responded out of fear, which was usually the same reason people stayed in abusive situations. The trainers and abusers don't have the trust or hearts of their partners.

Today Pat hoped to show something special—the staying power of a heart-centered relationship. He took a deep breath as he silently prayed. After positioning the horses side by side, he stepped on a pedestal next to Prophet, swung his leg over the bareback pad, and settled in. He squeezed his legs and cued Evangelist to move next to him. Pat placed his hands on each side of Prophet's shoulders, thrust his weight forward, and stood up on the pad. Both horses continued to walk in step with each other. To stand on both horses, Pat shifted all his weight onto his left foot so he could swing his right leg over to Evangelist's back. When Pat did so, the saddle pad under his left foot slipped sideways. He lost his balance and fell between the horses.

The crowd gasped.

The horses, however, never flinched but instantly came to a halt.

Pat landed on his feet. He reassured the crowd he was all right. Then he quickly stripped off the saddle pads and moved the horses back to the starting point.

Pat's heart raced as he used the pedestal to get back on Prophet. Pat again stood on Prophet's back. Holding his breath, he swung his leg over and placed his right foot on Evangelist's back. Pat's spirit soared as the horses stood perfectly still. Pat finished his message. "Whether we're a husband, or wife, or friends, we really need to keep Christ in the center of our relationships so they'll work smoothly and effectively."

· Prophet, Pat, and Evangelist ·

Evangelist and Prophet performed perfectly for the crowd because they wanted to please Pat. He'd captured their hearts and their trust. By watching and listening to Pat's cues, they constantly fine-tuned their timing, direction, and pacing to stay with each other. The unity between Pat and his horses reveals a secret to developing oneness with Christ and with each other.

First, it's essential to give our whole hearts to Christ and desire to do His will. Then God encourages us to develop unity with each other. "How good and pleasant it is when God's people live together in unity" (Psalm 133:1)! The apostle Paul wrote to the believers in Ephesus, "Make every effort to keep the unity of the Spirit through the bond of peace" (Ephesians 4:3). Once we do that, God becomes our Guide who gently shows us where and how to go. He will give us cues to keep us from going off course and share His wisdom for handling problems. But we need to stay alert and pay attention so we won't miss any signals.

After Pat's performance, there were several lasting changes made in the small community. For weeks the people talked about his message and the miraculous horses that loved and trusted him. They understood that God wanted them to love and trust Him so they could work together. God touched their hearts and worked through Pat's message to help them iron out conflicts.

But the biggest change was inside Pat's heart. He'd been willing to go out on a limb by listening to what God asked him to do—work the horses with no harnesses, reins, straps, or lead ropes. Then Pat had stepped out in faith to do what was possible only with God's help. Working in unity with God, Pat was blessed beyond his expectations. And the crowd was blessed to witness God at work in and through Pat and his horses.

Lord, show me how to live in unity with You
and other believers. Amen.

· Thoughts to Ponder ·

How has God been a gentle trainer directing you through life? How do you usually respond to Him? Have you given God your mind *and* heart?

38

THE SOLDIER

An Advocate

Saddles creaked as 24 men dressed in traditional 1870's blue cavalry uniforms, including tall black boots, stepped into the stirrups and slid into the old army saddles. Turning their horses, they left the lights of the barracks behind and rode into the semi-darkness of early morning. In the still air, hoofbeats rumbled the ground. Ted reached down and rubbed the neck of his horse before resting his forearm on the .45 Colt pistol he had strapped on his belt.

Ted's love of history had drawn him to ride in this reenactment of the Battle of the Little Bighorn, also known as Custer's Last Stand. But it was more than history that drew him. When he was a young child, he loved standing next to his parents on the flag-lined main street of Morris, Minnesota, to honor the veterans on Memorial Day. The heroes in Ted's world were the men and women who agreed to stand in harm's way and, if need be, give up their lives to protect others.

In September 1966, Ted became one of those people again. He rejoined the active navy, and within a year he became a photo officer for the U.S. Navy inside Vietnam. In 1968, he was sent to document a Navy SEAL's burial at sea. Ted stood holding his camera aboard the deck of a naval ship in the China Sea. The sun glistened off the calm water as the ship stopped moving. The U.S. flag hung at half-mast and soldiers wearing dress white uniforms commenced the ceremony. The flag-draped coffin was placed on a wooden plank that extended at right angles to the ship. At the appropriate time, the plank was tilted. In silence, the casket-bearers held on to the flag as the casket grated down the plank and splashed into the sea. For a couple of seconds it floated, but slowly it filled with water and sank. After the roar of the 21-gun salute and the sorrowful sound of Taps drifted away, only Ted's photos and grieving family and friends remained. The burial was etched deeply in Ted's memory, perhaps because most of the people for whom the navy man had died would never even know his name.

That day fueled a flaming desire inside Ted, a desire to protect the innocent and honor others who do the same. After leaving Vietnam, he served in law enforcement and is still actively involved in honoring veterans. Although Ted had ridden and owned horses throughout his life, he'd never ridden on a battlefield to honor the soldiers who had died so many years ago. That is why Ted and the men he was riding with were here now—to honor those who gave their all.

The beat of hooves striking the ground reverberated through the dawn. A solemn air hung over the troops as they rode single file up a tall hill. Ted's thoughts drifted to the previous days when he'd walked the grassy battlefield they'd be on today. Stark white grave markers dotted the field where soldiers had fallen—soldiers with antique weapons, no communication, and only their feet and horses for transportation. Clusters of white markers showed the intense areas of battle. The men who had died here had signed up to serve. They didn't have a choice as to where to go, what battles they would fight, or who their commanding officers would be. They'd been willing to give their lives for the United States—and they had.

An American flag gently waved above the soldier in the lead, who held the pole steady with his hand. The end of the pole rested on his stirrup. The second in line displayed the Guidon flag, a smaller red, white, and blue swallowtail flag of the Seventh Cavalry, also known as the "Guide." As the men on horseback topped the hill, they silently formed a line facing east. Reining in their horses, the soldiers waited for the sun to fully rise. Only the occasional creaks of saddles broke the silence. It was as if the horses knew this moment was sacred.

A cool Montana breeze carried the summer smells of fresh green grass and the sweet bouquet of prairie flowers. The men in blue uniforms sat astride their horses waiting. Men and horses almost looked like statues. The sun's rays poked above the horizon. A voice rang out.

"Draw your weapons. Prepare to fire blank ammo." In unison the men drew their pistols, many of them Colt .45s, the weapon most of the fallen soldiers had carried.

"Fire!"

Six times the guns roared in unison on command. The horses held their positions. After the last volley, each soldier held his weapon across his chest at parade rest.

As the sun rose, a bugler played Taps. The woeful sound drifted down the hill and across the dew-drenched meadows. For several minutes the reenactment soldiers watched the sun cast its golden light across the rolling hills. The man carrying the Guidon flag turned his horse and rode off. Next went the man with the American flag. As he turned, the flag gracefully waved. The rest of the men fell in line single file. Again only hoofbeats drumming the grass was heard.

I was intrigued when a friend told me about Ted and his ride. After I met him and got to know him a bit, I realized that what I admired was how Christ was reflected in Ted's everyday living. His passion is to be an advocate. He fought for freedom, was a voice for the innocent, and continues to honor his fellow soldiers. When Ted stands in the gap separating good from evil, he reflects Christ's nature. Jesus Christ is an advocate and defender: "If anyone does sin, we have an advocate who pleads our case before the Father. He is Jesus Christ, the one who is truly righteous" (1 John 2:1 NLT).

Have you needed an advocate? Have you been accused of doing something wrong? Have thoughts of defeat or shame attacked you? Did you know that the spiritual accuser is the devil? "Be alert and of sober mind. Your enemy the devil prowls around like a roaring lion looking for someone to devour" (1 Peter 5:8). Revelation 12:10 casts light on how deviously persistent the devil can be and tells of his future: "The accuser of our brothers and sisters, who accuses them before our God day and night, has been hurled down." Did you know that day and night the devil is accusing you of sin and telling God how unworthy you are?

What happens next is supernatural. In my mind, the scene plays out like an old-time John Wayne western. The bad guy—the one in the black hat—is bad mouthing someone. The sheriff steps in and says, "Hold on there a minute, Pilgrim." And he proceeds to straighten everything out according to the law. If we're born again, Jesus is the sheriff and advocate who steps in to defend us. He willingly died for us, giving His all to rescue us, defend us, and restore our relationship with God. Have you considered how powerful that is? God, in the form of Jesus, *personally* represents each one of us who choose to repent of our sins and call on His name for salvation.

• Ted getting ready to ride •

Knowing Jesus willingly defends me sheds new light on His love for me. He's truly my hero. Is He yours?

Lord, thank You for giving Your life to rescue me, defend me, and restore my relationship with You. Amen.

• Thoughts to Ponder •

How do you feel when you think of the devil accusing you of sins day and night before God? What might he be saying about you? Is it true? Have you repented of your sins and given your life to the Lord Jesus Christ? If you have and are living with Him as your Lord and Savior, the devil can accuse forever but he won't be heard. Your advocate, Jesus, stands between the devil and you.

39

THE CASTAWAY

Unwanted

The barn lights cast an eerie glow through the cold rain that drummed against the hood of Sharon's blue raincoat. Grunting, she pushed the full wheelbarrow to the manure pile outside the barn. After dumping it, she sighed and stopped to catch her breath. Floodlights illuminated the outdoor arenas and cast fingers of light through the pastures. Sharon cocked her head. In one of the wide rays of light and about 100 yards away was a ghostly outline of a horse. She squinted. The vapor from the heat of her breath mingled with the frigid winter air and floated in front of her eyes. She blinked in surprise. A white horse?

He stood in the cattle pasture where no horses were supposed to be. Sharon leaned forward, resting against the wheelbarrow. *What is he doing here? Whose horse is he?* The horse stood all by himself with his head hanging low. His tail was tucked in close, and he seemed hunched up as if he were freezing. *He looks too thin,* Sharon decided. *Could he be hypothermic? The cold rain is washing away his body heat. He won't be able to get warm until the sun comes out. He might be dead before then.*

Suddenly the horse lay down. Unable to get comfortable, he struggled to his feet again. His body teetered, almost as if he couldn't decide what to do. Then he put his feet together and sank back to the ground.

Alarmed now, Sharon wondered if he had colic. Pain in his gut would make him lie down and get back up again. Colic could kill him if he's left alone. *Whatever he is, he's in pain and needs help now!*

Quickly she pushed the wheelbarrow into the barn and put it away. She sloshed through puddles to the 100-year-old, two-story ranch house. Standing on the porch, she wiggled her muck boots over the boot scraper before stepping inside. Warm air enfolded her. She made her way down the hall to the office, her footsteps echoing off the tall ceilings and plastered walls.

The ranch manager sat behind a wooden desk. Streaks of gray highlighted his dark-brown hair. He glanced up as Sharon walked in.

Sharon rubbed her hands to warm them as she asked, "Do you know whose white horse that is in the cattle pasture?"

Joe rested his muscular arms on the desk and folded his hands. "It came in this afternoon with the load of cows I bought. The owners didn't want it, so they put it on the cattle truck."

Sharon shared her concern that the horse looked like he was in pain. He might be in danger of hypothermia or even colic.

Joe looked at her like she was droning on about a stray cat that had wandered in—the one no one wants to feed because then it'd stay. He tried to dismiss her concern with a shrug and a fatalistic attitude. "Sharon, the horse is either going to make it or it's not."

Sharon flushed and put her hands on her hips. "I'm going out there to put a halter on him and take him into the barn. I'll pay for the extra stall. I'm going to take care of him. No horse will suffer while I'm around."

Joe leaned forward and his brown eyes narrowed. "Do what you feel you have to, but you're wasting your time. I don't think you can pull that horse through."

Slipping on the hood on her raincoat, Sharon stomped out. She sloshed to the barn. Grabbing a halter she slung it over her shoulder. Slopping through the mud, she eased her way through the gate and out to the pasture. The rain slapped the ground and spattered mud on her jeans. When she got within 20 feet of the horse, she slowed her walk, not knowing what to expect.

She ran her eyes over him. The horse shivered violently, his head hanging nearly to the ground. His eyes were half closed. He was a bag of bones. His drenched fur accentuated his tautly stretched skin. Rain ran in rivulets between each protruding rib. Mud from lying down plastered his legs and belly. His hip bones protruded like knobs.

Sharon grimaced. *He's been starved so long he doesn't have any flesh on him to keep him warm. It's amazing he's even alive. How can anyone treat an animal like this?* With compassion, Sharon eased next to him. Slowly he opened his eyes and tried to focus his dull-looking eyes. Their gaze met, and sorrow pierced Sharon's heart. She sensed this horse knew he'd been tossed away but didn't understand why.

Taking the halter from her shoulder, she eased the straps open wide and held it under the horse's nose.

For a split second the white horse looked at the halter, his mind too cold and slow to comprehend. Then he obediently dropped his nose between the straps.

Gently Sharon buckled the halter. Grasping the lead rope, she lightly lifted it, encouraging the horse forward.

The poor guy struggled. As he stepped forward, he sighed.

Sharon led him through the gate, into the barn, and put him in an empty box stall. Grabbing towels from her tack room, she rubbed down the horse from head to tail. He was so thin it was like rubbing an old-fashioned washboard.

Even though he was still shivering and seemed to be in pain, the old boy kept looking back at her. He nudged her with his nose.

Sharon was sure he was saying thank you. Fierce determination rose inside her. No matter what, she was going to do everything in her power to bring this horse back to health. And then she was going to keep him.

The pile of soaking wet towels grew. Sharon wicked enough of the water and mud out of his coat to notice that he was really a leopard-spotted appaloosa. After bundling him in two fluffy horse blankets, she mixed up some hot mash and held it in front of him. She watched him weakly pick up pieces of grain and roll them in his mouth before swallowing them. She added more shavings to the floor, filled the water bucket, and tossed a couple flakes of hay in the manger. Satisfied she'd done everything she could, she said goodbye and drove home.

The next morning when she arrived at the stables, she went into the barn and looked over the stall door. The spotted horse nickered softly to her. He even had a glint of life shining in his eyes.

When Sharon shared this story with me, my heart ached. The barn was a busy boarding facility. There were a lot of people there who knew this horse was suffering and close to death, yet nobody else stepped in and offered to help. Why? Was it because it might cost them time or money or something else? Was it because the horse couldn't do anything in return for them? That there was no tangible reward for a good deed?

· Much-loved Sedona ·

Many years ago when I lived in Kalispell, Montana, I was driving my red-and-gray Dodge diesel pickup through town. My eye caught sight of a hunched-over man with a dirty beard and straggly gray hair. He was walking through the parking lot of a fast-food restaurant. Flung over his shoulder was a bulging, black-plastic trash bag. The stoplight in front of me turned red. My pickup's diesel engine surged as I downshifted.

I glanced over my shoulder at the man and noticed the torn and dirty rags he wore. I heard in my spirit, "Buy him lunch." I hesitantly thought, *Okay.* I knew I didn't have enough cash on me and the restaurant wouldn't take a check, so I replied out loud, "God, I need to get cash. If he's still here when I come back from the bank, I will buy him lunch."

When I drove back from the bank, the man wasn't in sight. That was okay with me. I almost flew on past the restaurant, but from deep in my spirit I heard, "Turn into the parking lot." I did, and sure enough the homeless man was standing by the Dumpsters adding to the treasures in his trash bag.

I pulled in close and jumped out of the truck. As I walked over, the man cowered, probably thinking I was going to yell at him or chase him away.

I smiled and said, "Excuse me, sir."

He looked over his shoulder, thinking I might be talking to someone else.

I continued. "Would it be okay if I buy you lunch?"

His dull eyes met mine. Dirty dreadlocks rimmed his sunken cheeks. He looked like he hadn't eaten a decent meal in years—or taken a bath. His layers of tattered clothing hung limply and his body and clothes reeked.

Squinting, the homeless man shrugged.

As I turned to go inside, I gestured for him to come with me.

Suspicious that I might have an ulterior motive, he kept his distance as we walked into the restaurant. When I asked him what he'd like to eat, he said, "One taco."

I ordered a dinner meal with six tacos, a drink, and potatoes, explaining to him that he could take the extra with him when he left if he wanted to.

From his deeply creased and sunburned face a small grin escaped, exposing broken and rotten teeth. His long, straggly, gray beard was streaked with yellow dribble from chewing tobacco, and his breath nearly gagged me.

I paid for the food and handed him the bag, intending to leave and get a deep breath of fresh air outside. But then I heard it. The instruction given to my spirit was "Sit with him while he eats." *Really? Ewww*, I thought. But I did as God directed.

We sat down at a table, and the man shoveled his first taco in his mouth. He wiped his face with the back of his hand and leaned forward. His beady eyes stared into mine. Under his breath he asked seriously, "Okay, who do you want me to kill?"

I blinked. "Kill?" I repeated. "I don't want you to kill anyone."

"Then why did you buy me this meal?"

My heart pounded. "Because Jesus told me to."

He chewed on his cheek and stared at me.

I shared that Jesus loved him, that Jesus cared for him, and that Jesus died on the cross for him.

The man stared at me and then looked down at the table. He poured out his heart. He was a Vietnam veteran who'd lost his family because of his drug and drinking habits. He'd been living on the street for decades. He wanted more than anything to be reunited with his son.

I shared that Jesus would forgive him of all of his sins and would give him a future. That all he had to do was ask Him.

The man shook his head.

My heart ached for him. I didn't want to leave, but it was time.

As we stood I asked, "Do you mind if I give you a hug?"

Tears rolled down his face, drawing lines through the dirt. His body shook as if he were trying to contain sobs. He swallowed hard and whispered, "Nobody's given me a hug for over 40 years."

I wrapped my arms around his bony, stinky body and cradled his head on my shoulder as he cried. In 30 minutes God had changed my heart. I'd been transformed from acting out of obedience only to acting out of God's love. And there's a big difference. With the latter, I didn't just give the man food; I gave him true compassion from the depths of my heart.

Why did I stop and help that man? I'd driven past beggars on the streets many times. *What was different this time?* I wondered. *God placed him on my heart,* I decided. This homeless man was a throwaway person according to the mores of today's society. He didn't have anything going for him—no job, a black-plastic trash bag full of junk that should have been left in a Dumpster, and bad choices he'd made and probably continued to make. In spite of all of that, God had compassion on him and wanted to draw him close.

God did the same thing with me…offering me the same compassion. I wasn't where that man was, but I could have been, and my sins were equal to his. A hard thought hit me. *If that man had been a homeless horse, I would have immediately opened my arms and heart wide and lavished it with love just like Sharon did for the castaway horse.*

But this man was filthy and stunk from his own choices, my mind countered. His situation was his own doing. Of course I wanted to be obedient to God, but all I wanted to do was swoop in, pay for his meal, and drive off.

When God had me sit down with the man in rags and listen, He helped me connect with the man's heart. I'm reminded of the parable of the Good Samaritan Jesus told. In the story Jesus defines what it takes to fulfill His command, "Love your neighbor as yourself." A Jewish man is robbed, beaten, and left for dead alongside a road. Many people walked past him, ignoring his plight. Some even moved to the far side of the street. But a Samaritan man (a race the Israelites despised at the time) stopped, dressed his wounds, and took him to an inn. He told the innkeeper to take care of the man and that when he returned he'd settle the bill (Luke 10:25-37). The man who acted from his heart with mercy was the one who fulfilled Jesus' teaching.

What I didn't realize was that God had a bigger plan. That day I fulfilled a divine assignment God had written on His calendar. After I left the restaurant, I couldn't get that homeless man off my mind. I prayed day and night for him. Then I discovered more of God's plan. Once a month my church served dinner at a homeless shelter. As I dished up roast turkey and steaming mashed potatoes, I felt a tap on my shoulder and heard a man's voice say, "Ma'am?" I turned around.

The man's eyes sparkled when he smiled. His parted lips revealed rotten and broken teeth. "You bought me dinner the other day." He stood a bit taller and was wearing clean clothes. His gray hair was washed, brushed, and tied back in a ponytail. Stroking his neatly trimmed beard he said, "I did what you suggested. I gave my life to the Lord." Tears welled up in the corners of his eyes, "And God's brought my son into my life. Tomorrow I take the bus to go see him."

We wrapped our arms around each other and cried happy tears.

I'd witnessed a miracle. God's love had transformed a castaway man—one who had nothing going for him—into a follower of Christ. Jesus had also helped me become more compassionate.

Sharon had witnessed a miracle too. As she invested hours of love into her castaway horse, his body and spirit recovered. He became a stunningly beautiful saddle horse she named Sedona.

God's love never fails. He's the perfect solution for all castaways.

*Lord, help me share Your love with people as easily as
I do with animals. Amen.*

• Thoughts to Ponder •

Has God asked you to be kind to an outcast? How did you respond? Did you act out of obedience or out of a loving heart? Have you felt like a castaway? God loves you and cares for you even if you've made some really bad mistakes. His arms are *always* open wide, waiting to forgive you and love you. He wants you to be a part of His family.

40

THE BIGGEST BLESSING

A Grateful Heart

The scrambling sounds of tiny hooves scraping my wooden kitchen floor jarred me awake. I shook my head and clicked on the light by my bedside. Sitting on the edge of my bed, I donned my slippers and pattered down the stairs. I flipped on the kitchen light. The three-day-old, lanky, brown mule foal stood in the kitchen inside a small area I'd fenced off. With her long ears pointed straight toward me, she squinted and blinked her long, black eyelashes.

I grinned. "Good morning, Little Girl."

The baby bobbed her head and nickered a greeting back to me.

I stepped through the little gate. Crouching next to her, I stroked her velvety hair. "You get to see your mama today."

The foal sniffed my nose, and her breath whispered across my cheek. I winced when I looked at her face. The hair along her entire jawline had been shaved for the surgery. The ragged edges of the stitches made her look like a Frankenstein creation.

The day before, when the foal had been playing on the rolling hills of the grassy pasture, she'd been accidentally kicked in the head by another horse. The impact had shattered her jaw. Her mother, Amy, had been sure her baby was dead and had abandoned her. At feeding time, the mare came in without the foal so a search followed. The foal was discovered a half mile away lying in a heap under a clump of sagebrush. The side of her face was bashed in from the impact. She was bleeding out of her ears, nose, and mouth. I scooped her up, put her in the car, and hauled her to the veterinarian clinic. I assisted the doctor in cleaning her up, putting a pin in her jaw, and then wiring her jaw shut. It was well after dark when I pulled the car into the driveway and carried the foal into the kitchen. I quickly set up a little enclosed area to keep her warm and safe until I could reunite her with her mom.

What happened the next day shocked me so much I've never forgotten it. On that blustery May morning I went out to the pasture and haltered Little Girl's mom, a gray Percheron mare. While walking Amy to the barn, her steps seemed unsure. She barely lifted her hooves, grating them against the gravel on the road. Her eyes were glazed over, her head hung low, and her lips drooped. She was mourning her baby. I couldn't wait to show her that her baby was alive. I walked her into the yard and tied her to a tree outside the kitchen door.

I skipped up the steps, walked into the kitchen, and gathered the baby into my arms. I heaved her off the ground. Little Girl's heart pounded as she struggled before she relaxed and rested in my arms. Waddling from the awkward weight, I carried her outside.

"Amy, look! It's your baby!" I called softly.

The mare ignored me; her eyes blank.

I raised my voice as I neared her. "Amy! Hey, Amy—look! It's your baby!"

But the mare never even flicked an ear. She stared at the bark of the tree she was tied to.

Using my knee I pushed up on the weight of the sagging baby to get a better grip. I shuffled next to the mare. Grunting, I lifted the 85-pound foal toward the mare's nose so she could smell her, hoping the scent would register in her brain.

Amy recoiled violently. She reared, and the muscles in her powerful body rippled. Pop! The halter broke. She pivoted on her hind legs and raced down the road back to the pasture.

I stood with my jaw dropped. *What is she thinking?* I wondered. In shock, I lugged the foal back into the kitchen. *The biggest blessing of Amy's life was right in front of her, and she didn't even see it!* My heart was crushed. I never expected the big gray mare to not recognize her own baby!

Later that day I confined the tall, dapple-gray mare inside a small lean-to shed that was built into a hill behind the house. I scooted the foal down the grassy slope and through the narrow wooden doorway. Amy had her head buried in the manger full of hay. When we entered, she raised her head and glanced at us. Gently I pushed the foal toward her. Amy stopped chewing. Strands of hay stuck out of her mouth as she reached out to sniff the little one. Her nostrils flared.

The foal recognized her mom and whickered.

Amy's eyes grew wide, almost like she'd seen a ghost. She buried her nose in the baby's coat and drew in a long breath. Hesitantly she whispered in a low voice.

Little Girl answered with a little squeal as if saying, "Yes, Mom! It really is me."

For the next half hour Amy licked her foal from her head to her hooves and chortled to her. The mare finally recognized her great blessing was alive and standing by her side!

When I remember Amy's inability to see the blessing I held in front of her, I'm reminded that oftentimes I'm as blind as she was. I forget the good things that surround me—even the simple things. Having a roof overhead and heat in my home. Having food to cook and put on the table. Having the ability to turn on a faucet and get fresh water. Many people in the world will never experience those things. My treasure chest of blessings also contains wonderful family and friends.

How can I forget that I'm so blessed? It happens slowly. When I focus on the disappointments in life, my vision gets cloudy. Just like Amy not being able to see through her grief of losing her baby, a dark veil of oppression envelops me until it feels like nothing else exists.

When that happens I feel akin to how the Israelites must have felt when God delivered them from slavery in the land of Egypt. Blessings surrounded them. Exodus 13:21-22 records, "By day the LORD went ahead of them in a pillar of cloud to guide them on their way and by night in a pillar of fire to give them light, so that they could travel by day or night. Neither the pillar of cloud by day nor the pillar of fire by night left its place in front of the people."

These miracles were evident 24/7. Instead of focusing on God and the land He'd promised, the Israelites chose to whine and be grieved by what they'd left behind. Even if they'd been only shortsighted, they could have concentrated on God's presence that billowed before them. But because they only saw the difficulties. They lost their grateful hearts. The long-term consequence was that they forfeited their blessing of entering into the Promised Land (Numbers 14:20-23). The people chose to grumble about the inconveniences instead of having faith in the blessings promised by God and fostering grateful hearts.

I counted my blessings every two hours around the clock as I milked Amy, poured the liquid into a bottle, and hand-fed Little Girl, which was difficult because of her jaw being wired shut. What a wonder to see the change in Amy. In those moments in the barn when she recognized her baby, her whole countenance changed. She proved to be an incredible and happy mother to Little Girl. The foal that looked like Frankenstein grew into a strong and healthy mule that carried my gear and provisions when I worked in the Bob Marshall Wilderness Complex.

Because of the broken jaw, Little Girl's nose curls off to the side like a "J," but that hasn't slowed her down. Now she's a senior who enjoys life as she and her companions eat grass in the pasture. Every day she reminds me that the key to a blessed life is cultivating a grateful heart.

Lord, when disappointments in life look overwhelming,
remind me to see the blessings that surround me. Amen.

• Thoughts to Ponder •

Have disappointments in life ever hung over you like a dark cloud? Have they overtaken you so they are all you think about or see? When your focus is on them, you're not able to fully experience the blessings of God. How can you cultivate a grateful heart?

41

PRETTY TERRIFIC JET

Turning Grief Around

Tammy felt like she was in a fog as she wiped down the dog kennel at the vet clinic to clean it out since the dog had been released. The last couple months had been a nightmare. Her wounded heart felt battered…and bloody…and stone cold. Every day when she walked through the door at work, the scent of medicine mingled with the odor of powerful disinfectant was a welcome relief. As the end of her shift neared, she dreaded going home to an empty house.

When she got home, everywhere she looked she was reminded of her only child, Laura. She would have graduated from high school a few months prior, but she'd died in April. The shock shook Tammy and her husband, Buddy, to their core. Tammy felt like a deer blinded by the headlights of an oncoming car—not knowing which way to run so remaining frozen in place. The roller coaster of emotions would ratchet to the top of a loop and then plunge into the depths of despair. The worst time of the day was when she got home at one o'clock in the afternoon. Buddy didn't get home until much later. Tammy hated those long, lonely hours. She felt like an empty shell. It was as if her life had ended too. She'd loved being a mom; it had been a dream come true. But now Laura was gone. *What am I going to do for the next 50 years without a child to raise?* she wondered. *And there's no possibility of having grandchildren now.*

She knew she needed to find something else—something totally different—to occupy her time and mind. But she wasn't interested in going to some kind of club or joining a group of people where she'd have to open her mutilated heart and be vulnerable. She closed her eyes. *Lord, help me get through this.*

As Tammy tidied up the kennel, her mind drifted through possibilities. She'd always loved horses but didn't know anything about them. She vaguely knew some folks who raised horses. Maybe she could help them out. When the equine veterinarian walked through the door that afternoon, Tammy asked about horses and was referred to a local stable.

Tammy's heart raced as she drove up to the stables. It was the first time she'd felt excited in months. The beauty of the rich, green Florida farmland soothed her soul. After being given a tour of the grounds and the big barn, she settled in to mucking stalls. A perfect job for her. She would stay physically active and keep her mind occupied until Buddy got home from work. While she forked straw, she glanced out the stall door and noticed three young horses romping in the outside paddock. She paused and watched them bounce around on their spindly legs chasing each other.

When they put the babies in the barn to feed them, two of the colts shared a stall. Tammy was asked to carry in a bucket of feed. The light-sorrel colt with a brush of white on his forehead cocked his head when he noticed the new person. Tammy gazed at "PT," short for Pretty Terrific Jet, who was around seven months old. His dainty whiskers wiggled as he tipped his head back and smelled her. His teardrop-shaped ears pricked at attention.

How can something be so adorable? Tammy wondered. She crossed the large stall. His small hooves shuffled through the wood shavings on the floor as he followed her. She dumped his ration into the feed bucket that hung on the wall. Even though he dropped his head into the bucket to eat, his gaze followed her every move.

Monday through Friday Tammy mucked stalls in the morning and fed horses in the afternoon. When she drove out to the barn she felt she was entering a different world where she was surrounded by the peaceful sounds and scents of horses. It was a long way away from the cold, cruel world that had taken her daughter. At the stables Tammy's heart could be at rest.

A few days into her new job she was out in the pasture where the young horses were kept. PT walked up behind her, nuzzled her black T-shirt, and begged for scratches. Tammy smiled and crouched down to be at his eye level. While she rubbed the colt, his brown eyes seemed to look directly into her shredded and hurting heart. He adored her. Days later, when she was hunkered down in his stall working, he rested his head on her shoulder. Tammy paused and turned. The colt was asking for her love. She wrapped her arms around his neck. Sighing, she leaned her cheek into his velvety-soft fur. Love rose in her heart. *Maybe this colt needs me.* Her world became consumed with nurturing and learning how to care for the young horse.

Three weeks from the time she started, Tammy sensed an ominous cloud hanging over her. She finished feeding the horses, picked up a curry comb, and walked back to PT's stall to groom him. It had been a day when everything she did reminded her of Laura. The memories clung like a web she couldn't shake loose. She slid the stall door open. The two colts were slurping down their food. PT's gentle eyes followed her as she crouched next to his chest to brush him. He rested his head on Tammy's shoulder. Tears dripped down her cheeks. Wrapping her arms around his neck, she buried her face in his mane and neck and sobbed. The colt tipped his head down, as if drawing her closer for a bigger hug. When he did that, Tammy's healing began in earnest. By giving her love to the colt, she opened her heart a crack, making it possible to receive the colt's love. Through the giving and receiving of love, the stronghold of grief was broken.

Tammy eventually bought PT, and she continued to work at the barn for quite a while. She's sure God placed her horse in her life to give her something to love and nurture during those horribly painful months when she was grief stricken. PT was God providing a stepping-stone to get Tammy on the path to healing.

Tammy's experience reminds me of a great Bible verse: "Love never gives up, never loses faith, is always hopeful, and endures through every circumstance" (1 Corinthians 13:7 NLT). Although for Tammy the hardest thing to do was to become vulnerable, it was through becoming vulnerable that love healed her from the inside out. When I reflect on that, it makes total sense. "God is love. Whoever lives in love lives in God, and God in them" (1 John 4:16). So by giving love away, we're living lives of love that overflow with God. And God is the One who heals.

Tammy and Buddy took their healing one step further. On their journey to becoming emotionally whole, they had a desire to share their story and encourage hurting teens with the message that no matter what challenges a person faces, they're not alone because God will see them through. After they finished one series of talks, 49 teens dedicated their lives to Christ!

Lord, when I'm grieving, open my eyes to opportunities to give Your love to those around me. Help me move forward and be healed in You. Amen.

• Thoughts to Ponder •

Have you been through a tough situation where your heart was deeply hurt? It might have been a friend who betrayed you, a divorce, or a death such as Tammy experienced. Did you consider finding a way to give away God's love to help you heal? What would that look like in your life? How could you do that this week?

42

THE WHISTLE

Being Delighted

slipped on my tall, black irrigation boots and headed out the back door. The horses and mules had been grazing for an hour on the rich spring grass, and it was time for me to call them back into their dry pen where they'd spend the rest of their day. I glanced up at the morning sun that was casting golden rays through the pale-blue sky as I strolled into the corral. In the pasture, drops of dew clung to tall sprigs of grass. The horses and mules watched me out of the corners of their eyes as they furiously grabbed their final mouthfuls. The green metal gate creaked as I swung it open. After tying it in place. I put my two little fingers together in my mouth and blew a shrill whistle.

My animals quickly raised their heads. SkySong raced toward me, his black mane and tail flowing. The others skipped into an all-out run. I grinned with delight as they thundered through the field. At that moment God spoke to my spirit. "I'm delighted when you run to Me." I paused. For some reason the idea of God being delighted short-circuited my thought process.

There are times that I've wondered if I'm bothering Him with my trivial stuff. Other times I've thought that maybe He just puts up with me. But "delighted"? After meditating and studying on that, I discovered this verse: "The Lord your God will delight in you if you obey his voice and keep the commands and decrees written in this Book of Instruction, and if you turn to the Lord your God with all your heart and soul" (Deuteronomy 30:10 NLT). I chuckled after I read that. *If God delights in me when I run to Him, I want to be the fastest horse in the stable and race to Him like I'm on the last turn at the Kentucky Derby.*

Lord, open my mind to Your thoughts and love. Amen.

• Thoughts to Ponder •

Do you think you're bothering God when you talk to Him? Do you believe He's too busy running the universe to pay attention to you and your problems? He's not! God delights in you. He loves to hear from His children!

43

SEEING WITH THE HEART

True Vision

The smell of medicines the veterinarian had used hung in the chilly November air. Tonya stood by the shoulder of her bay mare in a 12 x 16 box stall attached to a large riding arena. The 37-year-old woman stroked the bay's soft winter coat. In the last three hours Tonya's world had turned upside down. She professionally raised and trained thoroughbreds. This five-year-old mare was one of Tonya's prospects for competition and one of the last foals out of her original breeding bloodlines.

Tonya's stomach twisted as she ran her fingers over the mare's face, tracing the prickly sutures on the four-inch gash above Lady's right eye. The mare had gotten kicked in the head by another horse so hard that she'd been knocked unconscious and her skull fractured. The veterinarian had used ultrasound to detect stray bone fragments and dig them out of the wound.

The mare was breathing shallowly, and the swelling around her brain had caused her to go deaf and blind. The veterinarian hadn't been encouraging. He'd said he didn't know if the mare would live through the next couple of hours, much less regain her hearing and sight. After he packed up his instruments and left, Tonya wondered what she was supposed to do next.

Although Tonya had been born blind, her parents raised her the same way they would if she could see. One summer day at an amusement park, her parents lifted the three-year-old onto the back of a pony. Tonya threw a fit. There were two ponies—one that trotted and one that walked. Thinking she might be frightened, her parents had placed her on the slow horse. Tonya wanted on the fast one! By the time she was five, she loved sitting next to her grandfather in the stands at the Del Mar race track. Tonya loved hearing the excitement of the cheering crowd, the singsong voices of the announcers, and the horses thundering down the track.

Tonya's parents looked for something in which she could excel and build a fulfilling life. Although they weren't horse people, they recognized this was something their daughter loved. They purchased several horses for her through the years. They usually got snookered by horse traders and ended up with misfits, rejects, and difficult horses. But Tonya gleaned a lifetime of lessons by working with the troubled critters. Because she was blind, she couldn't rely on sight to deal with their dangerous behavior so she learned to train from her heart. Working with horses became second nature. She eventually carved out a niche as a professional rider and trainer.

Tonya took a deep breath. The veterinarian's advice swirled through her mind. He'd been adamant that she shouldn't go into the stall with Lady. Due to the brain swelling, the mare might be unpredictable and reactive. She could lash out by kicking, rearing, or even falling on Tonya. It was hard to tell the behavior a brain injury might cause. If something were to happen, Tonya's blindness would keep her from seeing it coming so she wouldn't be able to get out of the way. Tonya had strongly objected. "I'm the only one she'll trust under these circumstances."

The veterinarian replied, "At least have someone with you, so if you get hurt you'll have help."

Taking his advice, Tonya asked her mom to stand outside the stall. Now the stall door was slightly ajar so Tonya could escape quickly if need be. Gently stroking the mare's neck, Tonya knew Lady's recovery would depend on staying calm. If the horse freaked out, she could easily hurt or even kill herself.

Horses are prey animals, and one reason they tend to be flighty is their location at the bottom of the food chain. Other animals hunt and eat them—and the horses know it. Lady needed to feel safe so she wouldn't bolt and crash into the walls. She needed to learn how to get around safely. She'd have to learn a new skill set—how to feel her way around the stall and, later, around a corral. Tonya knew how frightening it was to blindly crash into walls. The young woman decided she'd be Lady's "seeing-eye person" until the horse adjusted. The biggest problem was trying to get Lady to understand what was going on.

Tonya stood next to Lady's left shoulder. Using her right hand she gently curled her fingers around the snap of the lead rope under the mare's chin so she could guide her head. In her left hand, she held the extra length of lead rope so she could give the horse room to move without having to be too close to her. With the lightest pressure possible, Tonya pulled the lead rope forward, encouraging the mare to move. Lady would need to trust Tonya totally to walk forward blindly.

The tall bay hesitated and then tentatively took a step. Tonya smiled and stroked the mare's neck. She shadowed the horse by stepping forward as well.

Lady held her head high, and her muscles were tense.

Tonya lightly tugged again. The mare shuffled her feet through the shredded paper bedding scattered on the floor. Tonya counted the steps until they were within a few feet of the wall. Tonya hesitated. If the mare didn't follow the cues and slammed into the wall, she would panic. Carefully Tonya held the rope in her left hand and placed her right hand four inches behind the mare's ears. She wanted Lady to obey the cue that meant "keep your feet in place but stretch your neck and head forward."

The mare stepped forward and smacked the wall with her nose. Shocked, she threw her head up, snorted, and lurched back a few steps.

Tonya stayed alongside, afraid that if she let go the mare would explode in fear.

Lady suddenly froze in place, her breathing shallow and hard.

Tonya stroked the mare's neck, the only comfort she could communicate to the blind and deaf mare.

In a few minutes Lady lowered her head, and her breathing slowed.

Once again Tonya cued her forward to within a few feet of the wall. Tonya stopped the mare. This time when Tonya put her hand behind Lady's ears giving the cue, the mare cautiously did it. She brushed the wall with her whiskers and then her nose.

Tonya's heart leaped with joy. *Lady gets it! She understands!*

After they turned 90 degrees, the mare's muscles relaxed. Tonya "showed" Lady the water bucket that hung from the wall and the feeder in the corner. At each turn, the horse stretched her neck and head and felt for the wall. After a couple laps, Tonya reversed directions. Finally she let go and stepped out of the way. She listened as Lady explored on her own. Tonya could hear her gently brush against the walls. The mare kind of tapped her feet as she walked around.

Tonya smiled, realizing that Lady was doing exactly what she'd done when learning how to get around without seeing. She knew Lady was making a mental map of the stall.

Throughout the next two-and-a-half months, Tonya served as Lady's eyes and ears. She planted a baby monitor in the horse's stall and kept the receiver with her so she could tell if Lady was in trouble. Many health battles were fought, and Tonya tackled each one using the same training method. She looked into Lady's heart to see what the horse needed, and then met her there with help and encouragement.

Tonya's gift astonishes me. I first heard about her through a friend who had hired her and couldn't quit talking about how her horse had been transformed through Tonya's gentle training methods. Tonya's approach simmered in my mind for days before I grasped why it was so effective. When you look into the heart of a horse, you can clearly see how to help it. In the situation with the injured mare, Tonya could relate to the mare on an even deeper level because she also was blind. She knew the fears Lady was facing and the hurdles she'd need to jump. She'd been there and done that. Because she loved the mare, Tonya was willing to invest the time into coaching her through the disaster and recovery.

· Tonya, Izze, and Lady ·

Under Tonya's care and guidance, slowly and miraculously Lady regained her hearing and eyesight. Two years later Lady gave birth to a healthy foal, Izze, that I had the privilege of meeting.

Tonya's story with Lady reminds me of the greatest trainer and coach of all time—Jesus Christ. He also has experienced what we have. "For this reason he had to be made like them, fully human in every way, in order that he might become a merciful and faithful high priest in service to God, and that he might make atonement for the sins of the people. Because he himself suffered when he was tempted, he is able to help those who are being tempted" (Hebrews 2:17-18). Because Christ became a man and experienced the trials of daily living, He knows what's going on deep inside us. He's been here and done that. He wants to share His wisdom and give us help so we can live happy, fulfilling lives.

I've always been overwhelmed by the thought that the God of the universe left His beautiful and comfortable home in heaven to come to earth and live with us. He knew humans would kill Him, but He came anyway. He didn't come for Himself—He came for you and me.

Because of His love for us, Jesus looks into our hearts to see what we need. Then He comes alongside us and coaches us, teaching us the cues that will keep us safe. "Don't hit that wall," He says. And if we don't listen and we bonk our noses, He's there to comfort us and encourage us to repent, turn the corner, and step forward again.

*Lord, please help me wrap my mind around the fact that
You lived on earth as a human being, experiencing the same
things that I go through every day so I know You can
relate to me on every level. Amen.*

• Thoughts to Ponder •

Jesus is an understanding and gentle coach because He's been where you are. How has He encouraged you to step beyond your comfort zone and trust His guidance? How has He warned you of danger? How will remembering these things help your relationship with Him?

44

THE LOVE METER

Sharing Love

The keys on Sharon's computer clattered as she typed the email. Pausing, she wiped a tear from the corner of her eye before continuing. "So I need to downsize. I'm considering selling Satin. Do you know of any good homes?" Sharon's heart ached as she hit "Send." Immediately, she was assaulted by doubts. *Oh, Satin, how can I do this to you? You're my dream horse. Will I find someone who loves you as much as I do?*

For years Sharon had dreamed of owning a unique breed of horse called Gypsy, which was short for "Gypsy Vanner." This horse breed originated in the United Kingdom and Ireland by the gypsies who carefully mixed draft breeds with athletic breeds to create a multipurpose horse they could ride and use to pull their colorful wagons. Gypsy Vanners can be a variety of colors, but they have a telltale genetic trait of "feathers" or long hair that grows down their legs and around their feet. The horse's large bone structure coupled with its athletic ability produces incredible strength and grace.

On an internet classified ad page, Sharon discovered a buckskin paint filly who was a cross between a Gypsy and a quarter horse. Immediately she called the breeder. After negotiating, she made payments until the filly was just over a year old.

The sun shone brightly the March day the filly was to be delivered. Sharon wrung her hands and kept peeking out the kitchen window of her ranch house outside of Mariposa, California. When a pickup pulling an aluminum stock trailer rattled down her driveway, Sharon raced out the door. The driver swung open the door of the trailer. Sharon's heart beat quickly.

The filly's body was the color of dark cream, and it looked like someone had dribbled white paint on her back that ran in wide stripes down her legs. Her forelock contrasted nicely with her tan ears tipped with black. Gracefully she arched her neck like a princess as she stepped out of the trailer. Her dark-brown eyes with long, black eyelashes gazed at her surroundings. Her nostrils flared as she inhaled the new smells.

· Satin ·

Tears streamed down Sharon's face as she wrapped her arms around Satin's neck. Satin relaxed into Sharon's hug.

But now Sharon was contemplating selling Satin. Resting her forehead in her hands, Sharon wondered, *Am I doing the right thing for Satin?* She'd dreamed of riding the mare and breeding her. Satin was nearly three years old—time to start training in earnest. But Sharon had suffered a health setback, and the doctors said she could no longer ride. She stood up and walked outside. Standing by the wooden rail fence, she watched Satin frolic in the green grass.

Suddenly Satin spied her master. She stopped and pricked her black-tipped ears. The sun glinted off her creamy coat. She whinnied and burst into a gallop. She ran full-blast toward Sharon, issuing low-toned nickers the entire way. She pranced to a stop.

Sharon ducked through the wooden boards and threw her arms around the horse's neck. Satin put her chin on Sharon's shoulder and pulled Sharon toward her chest, as if giving her a hug. Sharon's heart ached. *How can I find someone who will love you as much as I do?*

Later an email came in from a dear friend. "I know a woman who will love Satin with all her heart, give her the training she needs, and won't ever sell her." The friend went on to explain that Kim was a kind soul who had wanted a Gypsy Vanner her whole life. Sharon closed her eyes and prayed. "God, help me make the right decision."

Sharon contacted Kim, and they emailed almost daily. Cautiously, Sharon evaluated everything Kim said. She discovered that they were so much alike they even shared the same faith. The first time they talked on the phone, Sharon was drawn to the sound of Kim's sweet voice.

Before the end of the call, Kim sensed Sharon's hesitation. "Would you like to pray together?" she asked. After they said "Amen," Kim softly said, "If you sell Satin to me, she will always belong to both of us. I'll keep you updated, and you'd be welcome to come see her."

During their prayer time, God had impressed on Sharon that she was to do the best thing for the horse. Although it was a tough decision, she knew she needed to let Satin go. After they hung up, Sharon took a deep breath and walked out to the pasture. Satin's head came up, and she gave a low chortle. Her white mane flowed as she trotted next to the fence. Sharon slid between the wooden boards and stroked Satin's neck. "You're going to a new place. And there's going to be another horse there that will be your pasture pal. His name is Russell."

When Sharon decided to sell Satin, it was based on loving the horse more than what she wanted for herself. God had found the perfect home for Satin. Instead of simply being a sale, the process was more like an adoption.

Adoption is an amazing process that can be fraught with uncertainty. It would be so much easier if someone would invent a "Love Meter"—a tool that measured the capacity, intensity, and lasting power of a person's love. Wouldn't that be slick? No guessing, no wondering. Just plain facts that could be typed on an official-looking form with scores in different categories.

I'm sure Sharon would have jumped at the chance to use a love meter while her heart was torn over what she was to do. And how about if we could use one when we meet new people or when we're thinking about getting married? Wouldn't it be great to have certified guarantees?

But if we had love meters, we wouldn't need to rely on God. The risks of the unknown are some of the factors that keep us seeking Him. Two of my favorite verses are in the book of Proverbs: "Trust in the LORD with all your heart; do not depend on your own understanding. Seek his will in all you do, and he will show you which path to take" (3:5-6 NLT). Those verses hold the answer to everything we'll ever face. Sharon did that when she prayed and followed God's direction. What a miracle to be able to ask God Almighty for advice because more than 2000 years ago the greatest adoption took place. God's love meter registered out-of-this-world when Jesus came to this earth and died for all of us. Through Him we are adopted into God's family! "I will be a Father to you, and you will be my sons and daughters, says the Lord Almighty" (2 Corinthians 6:18). All we need to do is receive Jesus as our Lord and Savior (for more information, please read "Time to Hit the Trail" at the end of this book).

Are you wondering how Satin's adoption worked out? Sharon cherishes the memories from owning her dream horse, but most of all she's thrilled that she helped make Kim's dream come true. Kim has followed through on training Satin and regularly emails pictures and tales of their special moments together. Kim and Sharon feel they own Satin together. God's solution worked out perfectly!

Lord, when I'm facing tough life decisions, help me
remember that Your love meter overflows for me.
You always have the perfect solution. Amen.

· Thoughts to Ponder ·

Picture how a love meter would register if you hooked God up to it. Now do the same if you were hooked up to it. What would it register in regard to how much you love God? What can you do to improve your score?

45

THE BATTLE OF THE CINCH

Kindness

Summer 1955

Although the details have faded with the years and become more like impressions in Carolyn's mind, she vividly remembers the quarter horse mare named Betty.

A hot, dry breeze rustled the grass on the hillsides and carried the smell of sage through the meadows of a large ranch in Southern California. The sun was high in the sky. Some men and boys worked around the main barn doing chores. Standing next to the corral were two 12-year-old girls in ponytails and wearing plaid flannel shirts, blue jeans, and cowboy boots.

Kim excitedly chatted about the darling palomino colt they'd ridden over to see. Carolyn took a bite of a sweet pickle, and then wrapped the remaining piece in waxed paper and stuffed it into her left shirt pocket. Stepping next to the bay quarter horse mare she was riding, the girl flipped the stirrup over the saddle horn of the tooled, black-leather western saddle. She tugged on the latigo to tighten the cinch. As she pulled, the mare inhaled, filling her lungs with air so Carolyn couldn't get the cinch very tight.

Squinting her eyes Carolyn growled, "Betty, stop that!" The teen grabbed the latigo with both hands. Bracing her feet, she yanked as hard as she could but the strap barely moved. She heard Kim's saddle squeak as she mounted. *Kim always has to wait around for me because*

I can't get the cinch tight, Carolyn thought. She sighed and put the stirrup back down. Gathering the reins, she slipped the toe of her boot into the stirrup and bounced her weight up. Before she could swing her leg over, the heavy saddle slipped sideways. Quickly Carolyn stumbled down, barely keeping herself from falling.

Kim chuckled, partially out of embarrassment for her friend.

Carolyn flushed.

From behind her Carolyn heard one of the men come closer.

"You know she's blowing up on you, don't you?" He strolled next to her, his smile wide and his eyes twinkling, "If you give her an elbow to the gut, it'll pop that air out."

Carolyn looked up at him blankly.

"Give her an elbow as you pull that cinch. Let me show you." The guy straightened the saddle, grasped the latigo, and as he pulled, he stuck his elbow into the mare's side. The mare exhaled and he quickly pulled the cinch tighter by a couple inches. Grinning, he said, "Just like that."

Embarrassed and flustered, Carolyn said thank you and climbed into the saddle. The two girls rode down the dirt road. Although that method did work, Carolyn didn't like the idea of belting the mare with her elbow even though she realized it probably didn't really hurt Betty. After all, horses kicked each other when they were playing, and she couldn't possibly elbow the mare that hard. But she thought it was kind of disrespectful. What else could she do?

The battle of the cinch had started the first time Carolyn hefted the heavy saddle onto Betty's tall back. Although she'd pulled the cinch as tight as she possibly could, the saddle slipped every time she put her foot into the stirrup. At first she thought she was doing something wrong—and maybe she was. This horse thing was new to her. But Betty had figured out that if she took a big breath of air and held it, the cinch couldn't be tightened as much. Carolyn had quickly learned to cinch the saddle, wait a minute or two, and then pull the latigo a bit more. It would tighten enough so she could mount, but 100 yards down the road when she asked the mare to speed up, the saddle would roll and Carolyn would slide to the ground.

Other than the cinch issue, Betty was a fine horse. Carolyn decided to give the elbow jab a try, and over the next couple of months she per-fected it as well as a petite 5'2", 100-pound gal could. But she still hated bonking her mare. Every time she did it, something scratched at her inside. She reasoned, *What other choice do I have? It's too dangerous to ride on a saddle that rolls under a horse's belly.*

Throughout the summer the battle of the cinch raged. On the days when Carolyn couldn't get the cinch tight, she'd strip off the saddle and ride bareback. Then one hot, summer day things changed. As usual, nosy Betty followed her around the corral as Carolyn cleaned it. Car-olyn stopped for a break and pulled a sweet pickle out of her pocket. Unwrapping the waxed paper, she nibbled on it and rewrapped the rest. She stuffed it into her pocket and went back to work. The next time she took a break, she took another bite of pickle, but this time she set the pickle on a wooden fence post, figuring she'd get back to it. When Carolyn turned around a few minute later, the pickle was gone!

She looked around and spied her bay mare on the other side of the corral chewing on something. Carolyn chuckled. The following day, Betty nudged Carolyn's pocket and they shared the pickle. The mare quickly became a sweet pickle addict. By fall, Carolyn's mother was get-ting a little irritated. There were five kids in their household, and she couldn't seem to keep any sweet pickles in the refrigerator.

One beautiful fall day, Kim and Carolyn planned to go horseback riding. Betty bloated up like a whale. Even with the elbow-bashing trick, Carolyn couldn't get the cinch tight. She was almost ready to ditch the saddle when Betty's nostrils suddenly flared and her whiskers wiggled. She curled her neck and nudged Carolyn's pocket. Grinning, Carolyn got out the pickle and broke off a piece for Betty. Then she got a brilliant idea. She set the piece of pickle in the palm of her left hand and grabbed the latigo with her right one.

When Betty stretched her lips and plucked the pickle into her mouth she let out all the air she'd been holding in.

Quickly Carolyn tugged the cinch tight.

Betty just enjoyed the treat, drooled, and smacked her lips.

This was the first time Carolyn had been able pull the cinch tight in one easy tug! Finally she'd discovered a solution that didn't involve force. She could give Betty something nice and sweet each time instead of poking her with her elbow. And the results were a lot better. From that day forward, Carolyn always went horseback riding armed with a sweet pickle.

When Carolyn emailed me a short note about her sweet pickle-eating horse, I laughed. I'd never heard of such a thing, but it made so much sense. The first thing that went through my mind was the advice my mother gave me as a little girl when I'd come into the house wearing a mad attitude because I was cross with a neighborhood friend. Mom's blue eyes would twinkle and she'd say, "You catch more flies with honey than vinegar." In other words, if I acted out of a loving heart and used sweet words rather than being bitter, resentful, or mad, the people around me would be drawn to me and together we could solve any challenges we faced.

As I got older, there were many times my life would have traveled down a more pleasant road if I'd applied Mom's wisdom. Eventually I discovered that Mom's wisdom was gleaned from the Bible. Proverbs 15:1 says, "A gentle answer turns away wrath, but a harsh word stirs up anger." That gentle answer could very well be a kind deed, such as sharing a sweet pickle. Proverbs 12:18 promises, "The words of the reckless pierce like swords, but the tongue of the wise brings healing."

Carolyn's heart's desire was to be kind to her horse, so when she discovered that sweet alternative, she quickly abandoned the elbow thumping. It's my heart's desire to speak encouraging, constructive words that convey God's love and grace. Perhaps I should wrap a sweet pickle in waxed paper and tuck it into my shirt pocket as a reminder.

Lord, when I'm having difficulty with people, open my eyes to some positive options for dealing with the situation. I want my relationships to thrive and honor You. Amen.

· Thoughts to Ponder ·

Do you have any difficult situations you're facing right now? How can you employ the "sweet pickle principle" to ease the tension?

46

THE GREAT ESCAPE

The Gift of Freedom

The light, spring breeze carried the scent of lush green grass past the small ranch house that was built on a hill above a creek that flowed through the Cypress Hills. Across the creek a barn stood with wooden corrals built around it. From the lawn, Claire lifted her hand, shielding her eyes from the sun as she watched her husband walk toward her. Ross had finished his morning chores and was coming in to eat lunch. She yelled, "The horses are out!"

Ross exploded. "No way! I'm going to have to start tying all the gates shut!" Over the last few days the horses had repeatedly escaped the corrals. The only time he kept horses in the corral was when he was riding every day. It was much faster and easier to grab one this way than going out into the enormous pasture to catch a horse. He always made sure they had plenty of food, water, and salt. The horses weren't getting out because their needs weren't being met.

Over lunch Ross and Claire discussed the great escape. They came to the conclusion that one of the horses had learned how to open the gate and enjoyed the challenge of doing it. They agreed to watch the corrals closely to discover which horse was the culprit.

One day Ross walked into the ranch house with a grin on his face. After washing up, sitting down, and scooting his chair under the table he shared his story.

"Yep! The culprit is Brandy. That horse is too smart for her own good!"

Brandy was a bay mare that had been born and raised on the ranch. She was a great all-around workhorse. Ross chuckled as he explained.

"Do you know what she did? That horse put her rear to the gate and rubbed until her tailbone got caught in the hand pull." He laughed in amazement. "She rubbed and gradually increased the sway in her hips until the board slid back. With immense satisfaction she turned around and watched the gate swing open. The herd thundered past her. She was the last to leave. I'm sure she was swinging her head side to side as she enjoyed her victory. We're going to have to tie the gates shut. What a nuisance!"

Brandy's antics remind me of a mule I knew from my backcountry trail-riding days. The tall, blocky sorrel got his name from his nose. The crew dubbed him "Parrott." Below his eyes his nose curled toward his chest, resembling a bird's beak. "Gentle" and "being willing to work" were his two best assets. His worst trait? He should have been named Houdini after the great magician who had a reputation for being able to escape out of anything. If Parrott decided he wanted to go somewhere, he figured a way to get out and do it. But escape wasn't enough for him. He had such loyalty to the other horses and mules that he made sure every single one of them got loose too.

Although it may sound funny now, it wasn't when we drove to the "end-of-the-road" corrals to get set up to take guests on pack trips into the mountains. We'd get there and discover there weren't any horses or mules in sight. We'd check, and sure enough the slide rails across the corral opening had been pushed away. The stock had thousands of acres of forest service land to wander in. We'd follow their tracks and catch them one by one. By the time we caught the stock, saddled up, and loaded the mules, the day was half over.

That night we sat around the campfire and decided to use baling twine to tie the three horizontal gate rails in place.

The next time we arrived for a pack trip, we found three broken rails and an empty corral.

When we returned from that pack trip, we put the animals in the corral and then hid in the woods. We spied on Parrott as he performed his great escape. We were amazed as we watched his technique.

Balancing both front feet on the bottom rail, Parrot leaned his weight back on his haunches. He reared and then crashed down, making sure his front feet hit the rail, snapping it in two. Then the big guy flopped to the ground. A cloud of dust enveloped him as he lay on his belly and scooted under the top two rails. Like I mentioned, he could have kept going, but he wasn't that selfish. He wanted to give his friends freedom too. When going under the rails, he stopped when the top rails were centered above his back. Then with a low grunt he jerked to his feet and snapped the two top rails. After that he'd stepped to the side and watched his friends take off. We were sure he had a grin on his face when he joined them.

Once Parrott mastered the gates, he went on to bigger and better things. He became like an old-time outlaw who insisted on breaking his friends out of jail. One morning at the end-of-the-road camp, we were within minutes of riding the trail for a summer pack trip. As part of the crew, I was talking with the guests and giving last-minute instructions for the trip. Unknown to us, Parrott was planning a massive escape.

Under the shade of some tall pines, the horses were saddled and tied to a hitching rail. With one back leg cocked, each one of them was peacefully napping. On the other side of the rail, the mules were laden with white packs filled with gear and food. They stood relaxed and sleepy as they bided away the time. That is, all the mules except Parrott.

Using his lips like fingers, that mule manipulated his lead rope until it was untied. Once again, he didn't stop there. Having mastered this new craft, he untied every horse and mule within minutes. The herd must have been overjoyed because some dropped their heads and ate the green grass while others frolicked around enjoying their taste of freedom. Those of us on crew were not impressed.

By the end of the summer, Parrott had become the herd's hero and the crew's main antagonist.

That big red mule was sure loyal to his friends. He insisted on giving them a taste of freedom whenever he could. I wonder what our world would look like if all Christians insisted on doing the same thing? The deepest bondage known to mankind isn't slavery, an oppressive government, or even prison. It's the bondage that the devil has over those who don't know or believe in Jesus Christ. The apostle Paul encourages us to get involved. "Gently instruct those who oppose the truth. Perhaps God will change those people's hearts, and they will learn the truth. Then they will come to their senses and escape from the devil's trap. For they have been held captive by him to do whatever he wants" (2 Timothy 2:25-26 NLT).

The scariest and most horrible thing is that the devil's bondage doesn't end when people die. No, his torture continues on as eternal torment in hell (Luke 12:4-5). There's only one way to be truly free from Satan's bondage: Accept the gifts of salvation, eternal life, and everlasting love offered by Jesus through His death on the cross. And that isn't complicated. The only thing people have to do is ask Jesus into their lives and let Him be their Lord and Savior. After that, Jesus will show them how to follow Him. (Read "Time to Hit the Trail" at the end of this book for more information.)

The process doesn't end there. Once we're free, we don't want to be selfish. Like Brandy and Parrott, we love our families, friends, and even strangers enough to show them the way to freedom too.

Just think about it. What would the world look like if each one of us shared the gift of freedom through Jesus with the people around us?

> *Lord, thank You for the freedom You've given me.*
> *Show me how I can be a jail breaker*
> *and help others escape bondage too. Amen.*

• Thoughts to Ponder •

Do you have any family members, friends, or acquaintances who don't know Jesus Christ personally? Do you love them enough to overcome any shyness or uneasiness about sharing the gospel? If you're worried about what to say, ask God to give you the wisdom and words you need. There are also multitudes of studies and classes you can take on sharing the gospel.

47

THE AUCTION

Ransomed

In south-central Georgia the auctioneer's singsong voice echoed through the old auction barn. Enormous ceiling fans circulated the 95-degree humid and stale air that was punctuated with the sour smells of cattle, goats, horses, and the body odor of hot and sweaty people packed inside elbow to elbow. Ann, some of her friends, and her 12-year-old daughter, Bri, sat on folding chairs in the front row beside the sale ring. They liked to get there early so they could get a close-up view of the horses being offered.

Ann enjoyed her "girl time" at the Saturday auctions, not because she wanted to buy more horses (she already had 10 at home) but because the exciting atmosphere resembled a craft fair and flea market.

The auctioneer's voice droned on as a mare and a colt trotted around the ring. Not paying attention, Ann and company chatted among themselves. In the background they heard the auctioneer holler out, "Sold!" The mare and colt were ushered out. Next a young, bay-roan stampeded in, capturing their attention. The whites of the mare's eyes showed as she raced around the arena looking for an escape route. It was obvious she hadn't been handled much and probably didn't have much training. Every rib showed. A fresh cut glistened above her eyes. Skinned up spots lined her legs. Ann was afraid the horse had been beaten to make it load into a trailer.

The air billowed with dust being churned up by the now trotting mare. Suddenly she stopped. Every muscle in her skinny body seemed to quake in fear. Overhead, the large fan blades slowly turned, barely moving the stifling air.

The auctioneer's voice rang out time and again asking for bids, but no hands were raised. In his rolling voice he kept lowering the price, trying to get an opening bid. Finally he sang out, "Five dollars. Can anyone give me five dollars?" A lanky cowboy, who looked to be in his twenties, raised the white card with his auction number. Ann was relieved. She was acquainted with Teddy and knew that he usually bought horses, trained them, and resold them. The auctioneer picked up his pace. "Ten dollars! Do I hear ten dollars?" But his plea settled on deaf ears. Nobody wanted the straggly, beat-up horse. "Sold for five dollars!" he announced.

After all the horses had been run through the ring, Ann and her group drifted to the back of the barn where the stalls were. They leaned into an enclosure holding a fuzzy baby donkey, chattering about how cute it was. A teenager skipped down the alleyway to her new horse. Her mom lagged several steps behind. As the woman passed Ann's group, she pointed to the straggly mare that now stood in a stall across the aisle. "Did you know that man bought her for slaughter?" she asked sadly.

Ann blinked. In shock, all the gals looked at each other. Forgetting the cute donkey, they walked over to the mare's stall. The horse watched them suspiciously. Hesitantly Ann opened the gate, stepped in, and closed the gate behind her. She held out her hand and murmured quietly to the horse.

The mare shied away and stood off to the side as far as she could, her body braced for action. Dried sweat crusted her neck. Slowly, Ann stepped toward her.

The mare stretched her neck and sniffed in Ann's direction.

Ann waited until the mare relaxed. Taking another step, Ann gently reached out and stroked the horse's neck.

The mare's tense muscles rippled but gradually relaxed as her fear ebbed.

Ann glanced over at her friends and daughter.

Bri was leaning over the wooden gate. She tucked a long strand of blond hair behind her ear. With sad eyes she pleaded, "Momma, let's buy her. Let's save her life."

Ann shook her head. "Bri, your daddy wouldn't go for it. We can't bring this horse home with us. It's not broke, and we've already got so many horses now."

Bri's eyes clouded over and tears welled up. "But, Momma, we can't let her go to slaughter."

The mare leaned into Ann's hand begging for more scratches.

Ann shook her head. "Bri, we can't do it. She's not broke."

Bri paused, deep in thought as she mentally added up her life savings—$15. "Momma, I've got my own money. I'll pay for her. I can't let her go to the slaughterhouse."

Ann hesitated and looked at the horse beside her. The mare was enjoying the attention now and acting like a normal horse instead of a crazy one.

Bri begged again. "Please, Momma! I'll pay for her with my own money!"

Ann sighed. "Go find Teddy and see if he's willing to sell her to you."

Bri raced through the crowd and headed toward the arena. Her heart thumped in her chest. *What if Teddy won't sell her?* From the first moment she saw the mare shivering with fear, she'd wanted to help her but didn't know how. This was her chance. She spotted Teddy's tall, wiry frame. He wore a T-shirt, blue jeans, and cowboy boots. She walked over to him.

"Mr. Teddy?" she asked.

He looked down at her. "Yes?"

"I–I–I'd like to b–buy the little b–bay-roan horse. I'll g–give you five dollars for her."

He hesitated.

Bri held her breath.

Finally he shrugged his shoulders. "Give me ten dollars, and you can have her."

Bri raced to her mom and explained the situation. Then she said, "Momma, I've got the ten dollars at home. I'll pay you back if you'll lend me the money now so I can buy her. Will you?"

Ann stroked the mare's forehead and nodded. "I'll call your daddy and have him bring the horse trailer so we can take her home."

Bri had gone the extra mile to buy a mare nobody wanted. She was scared, skinny, unruly, and beat up. But Bri saw something nobody else did when she looked into the horse's heart. She was willing to pay the man every dollar she had.

After getting her home, Bri named the mare Starlet. As Starlet settled in and experienced being handled with love and care, she became less fearful. In fact, Bri has been training her to be her saddle horse.

· Bri and Starlet ·

I'm so glad Bri saved Starlet. People are wrong when they decide an animal or person is worthless. That day Bri revealed and modeled God's love. When the people on earth were infested with sin, when we weren't worth much (if anything), God reached out to save us and offer us a home with Him. "God demonstrates his own love for us in this: While we were still sinners, Christ died for us" (Romans 5:8). That verse pierces my heart. God didn't wait for us to get our act together before sending Jesus to save us. He knew we couldn't change without His power living inside us. Jesus understood before He came that His earthly journey would be extremely difficult, but He came anyway. He chose to suffer for us. He was given 39 lashes—the maximum number without killing someone. The whip probably consisted of many leather strands with pieces of metal and bone tied to the ends. Every stroke would have ripped flesh from His body. Battered, bleeding, and bruised, He was forced to walk to Golgotha dragging the crossbeam he'd be hung on. His agony was visible as the nails pierced His flesh. Many people watched His struggle and scorned and ridiculed Him.

He went through this suffering to pay for our sins because He had never sinned. He ransomed us from spiritual death so we could be reconciled with God and have new life in Him.

Jesus died on the cross for you. Have you accepted His gifts of salvation, eternal life, and love?

Lord, open my eyes to the gifts You've given me,
especially the gift of salvation. Amen.

• Thoughts to Ponder •

Have you thought about the price Jesus paid for you? He willingly died because He loves you. Accepting Jesus and making Him your Lord and Savior isn't complicated or hard. You just need to acknowledge your failings (sins), repent, ask God to forgive you, and ask Jesus to be your Lord and Savior. This will be the best decision of your life!

48

TIME TO
HIT THE TRAIL

Does your life feel empty? Are you surviving instead of thriving? Perhaps you're trying to fill the void through sexual encounters, drugs, or alcohol. The hollow, nagging feeling won't disappear that way! God created you with a place in your heart that only He can fill. He loves you and wants you to be an active member of His family. There's only one way to do that: accept Jesus Christ as your Lord and Savior. Jesus said, "I am the way and the truth and the life. No one comes to the Father except through me" (John 14:6-7).

When I talk with people about accepting Christ, they often say they aren't good enough. And that's true! "All have sinned and fall short of the glory of God" (Romans 3:23). That's why God sent Jesus. He knew you couldn't change and grow spiritually strong without a personal relationship with Him. When you allow Jesus to become your Lord and Savior, He enters your heart and His power lives inside you. So what does God want you to do specifically? First, realize that you aren't perfect. Acknowledge that you need Him and want to give your life to Him. He loves you! He wants you to love Him back, but He lets you decide.

> If you declare with your mouth, "Jesus is Lord," and believe in your heart that God raised him from the dead, you will be saved. For it is with your heart that you believe and are justified, and it is with your mouth that you profess your faith and are saved (Romans 10:9-10).

Are you hitting the trail with God? Have you asked Jesus into your heart as your Lord and Savior? Or perhaps you've accepted His offer but have fallen away from Him. To invite Jesus into your life or to dedicate your life to Him, read this prayer from your heart:

> *Lord Jesus, I'm a sinner. I know I can't save myself. I believe You died on the cross for my sins. I believe You rose from the dead three days later and are with God in heaven. I accept Your offer of salvation. Please forgive all of my sins. Come into my heart and be my Lord and Savior forever. I trust You, and I love You! Amen.*

Welcome to the family of God! Now find a Christian and share your great news! Locate a Bible-based church to attend so you can continue to learn about God and grow in Him. I'm so excited for you! I encourage you to be in fellowship with God daily. Talk to Him, listen to Him, and read His Word.

With love in Christ,

Rebecca

· My friend, I pray that you ride with Jesus every day! ·